Turning Leaves

Richard Chalfen

Turning Leaves

The Photograph Collections of
Two Japanese American Families

University of New Mexico Press
Albuquerque

Library of Congress Cataloging-in-Publication Data

Chalfen, Richard.
   Turning leaves : the photograph collections of two Japanese
American families / Richard Chalfen. — 1st ed.
   p.   cm.
Includes bibliographical references and index.
ISBN 0-8263-1242-X
ISBN 0-8263-1243-8 (pbk.)
   1. Japanese American—Families.   2. Photograph collections—
Social aspects—United States.   1. Title.
E184.J3C47   1991
305.8'956073—dc20   ⁻
90-43793
CIP

For Leah and Claire

Contents

Acknowledgments

This book is the result of a considerable amount of cooperation over a period of years, and many thanks are due to a lot of people. First and foremost I want to mention the intellect, hard work, persistence, artistic abilities, and communication skills of Lynne Horiuchi. I met Lynne in Santa Fe, New Mexico, while I was on sabbatical, finishing the first draft of a book that summarized some of my previous work on home-mode communication. This writing included the development of communication models that incorporated amateur pictorial forms such as snapshots, family albums, home movies, and home videotapes. To that date, my work had been limited to examples drawn from personal observation of Anglo Americans living in the northeastern United States and only a few miscellaneous, often anecdotal, accounts from societies in other parts of the world. The book that resulted from this work, *Snapshot Versions of Life* (1987), implies that much more could be learned from cross-cultural studies of home-mode materials, and that we were only in the infant stages of such research and understanding. The Japanese American Family Album Project could not have been better timed.

During the summer of 1981, Lynne was in the midst of background research for a pilot project involving Japanese American family photography sponsored by the California Council for the Humanities. In the fall, she invited me to join her staff in Los Angeles to continue work on a new planning grant she had received from the Museums Division of the National Endowment for the Humanities. This was my introduction to the Nagano family and their rich collection of photographic materials. An exhibition, entitled *Japanese American Family Albums: A Los Angeles Family,* opened at the Japanese American Culture and Community Center in Los Angeles on February 20, 1983.

Shortly thereafter, I was asked by Elizabeth Akiya Chestnut to serve as project consultant on visual anthropology for the completion of a parallel pilot project in New Mexico. This work was primarily sponsored by the New Mexico Humanities Council. Some additional funds were provided by Lynne's NEH planning grant since there were already plans to combine, compare, and contrast materials from both California and New Mexico. This second opportunity provided me with a basic familiarity with the Uyeda/Miyamura families and their materials as researched and organized by Don and Sue Rundstrom. This work resulted in an exhibition entitled *Turning Leaves: Photographs from Japanese American Families in Gallup, New Mexico* which opened on March 4, 1984, at the Maxwell Museum of Anthropology located in Albuquerque at the University of New Mexico.

According to the original plan, Lynne and several consultants proceeded to complete and submit a proposal for an implementation grant from the Museum Division of the National Endowment of the Humanities. This third effort suggested a project that combined the two pilot projects and extended our findings with additional library research and continued fieldwork, interviewing, observation, and writing. The culmination of this effort resulted in a traveling exhibition that opened at the Lowie Museum of Anthropology, on the Berkeley campus of the University of California, on February 14, 1987. At this writing, the exhibition is scheduled for six sites on both east and west coasts through 1990.

Lynne served as project director. More important, she had the intuitive wisdom to foresee the significance of this effort. She genuinely felt the need to demonstrate in exhibition form the lasting and irreplaceable value of personal photograph collections to Japanese American families and to members of the community at large. Her intuitions have been so right on so many matters. Lynne's energy and dedication carried staff members through some difficult deadlines and controversial personality conflicts that inevitably accompany projects as complicated and extensive as this. I will forever be indebted to Lynne for asking me to serve as staff visual anthropologist.

This work would not have been possible at all without the enthusiastic cooperation of the Japanese American families who became the center of our project. Members of both the Nagano and Uyeda/Miyamura families were very generous with information about their personal lives—they shared their photographs, their memories, and their stories with us. Their willingness to state personal and even intimate thoughts, feelings, and beliefs provided us with the basis for what we have been able to accomplish. From Los Angeles, we are especially indebted to Steve Nagano, Paul Nagano, Tyrus Nagano, and Junko Nagano; and from Gallup, Chiko Miyamura Herrera, Hershey and Terry Miyamura, Michiko Yoshida, Grace Uyeda, and Kay Taira. Their permissions, cooperation, and, indeed, patience with us as we asked so many questions allowed this project to go forward. All photographs in this book belong to members of these families, and we are grateful for permissions to use them. All negatives made to reproduce these images are now part of an archival collection sponsored by the National Endowment for the Humanities.

We had a superb collection of project consultants who offered time, interest, energy, and professional expertise on our research whenever asked. These people include John Adair, Akemi Kikumura, Lloyd Inui, Robert Smith, John Collier, Jr., and Sue Embrey. Several of these people continued to read drafts of this monograph as I attempted to bring some unity to all that we had attempted to accomplish. In earlier phases of the overall project we had the help of Mari Lyn Salvador, Don and Sue Rundstrom, and Betty E. Mitson. Our research assistants and graphic assistants proved invaluable, especially Rosanna Hemerick, Dennis Markham, Steve Nagano, Glenna Oshima, Steve Perkins, Robert Tinana, Mary Ann Vallez, as well as Sonia Chan, Steve Sechovecs, and Daniel Simmons.

Generous thanks are extended for financial support from the Humanities Projects in Museum and Historical Organizations Division at the National Endowment of the Humanities. In particular we acknowledge the logistical guidance, intellectual support, and spiritual encouragement of Anna Caravelli and Sally Yerkovich, and later, Marsha Semmel. I also want to acknowledge staff support from the Japanese American Citizens League, the Japanese American Cultural and Community Center, the Maxwell Museum of Anthropology, and the Lowie Museum of Anthropology.

I am indebted to the College of Arts and Sciences of Temple University for granting me an academic study leave during the spring semester of 1987. This support offered me uninterrupted time for additional research and the opportunity to complete the first draft of this monograph. Thanks are also due to the Faculty Senate Research Committee at Temple for a grant-in-aid of research that helped defray the costs of preparing the photographs for publication.

I want to acknowledge the contributions of writing and editorial comment by Lynne Horiuchi, Elizabeth Chestnut, and Malcolm Collier. They have been very generous with their ideas, perspectives, insights, and support. I also extend my warm thanks to Dana Asbury and Milenda Lee at the University of New Mexico Press for their expertise and patience while guiding my manuscript toward publication. And finally the editorial assistance of Karen Donner must also be mentioned. She suffered through the awkward syntax of my previous book and has been very patient once again. I hasten to add that all errors in this book are my responsibility, the results of not having listened better to sound counsel.

RMC
Philadelphia

Preface

If ordinary people were asked to consider how photography might be related to Japanese Americans, most people would probably draw upon all too familiar stereotypes associated with Japanese people, not Japanese Americans. For instance, the first and most common image is that of a camera-carrying tourist from Japan, traveling in a group, snapping pictures of everything in sight, taking many pictures of themselves. This person, probably a man, might even be using more than one camera. In fact, our research uncovered an example of a Japanese tourist being asked to travel with several cameras belonging to his relatives and friends—he was meant to take pictures for them with their cameras. These photographs fulfilled the expectation that he would return home with presents for friends and relatives.

A second thought might refer to the popularity and excellent reputation of cameras produced by Japanese manufacturers and their longstanding availability in the American marketplace. Or, for people who have some knowledge about either patterns of Japanese immigration or examples of portrait photography, the "picture bride" phenomenon may come to mind. In Japan, *omiai* was the process by which a prospective bride and groom were introduced to one another and respective families through a series of ritualized meetings and interviews. After the introduction of camera technology into Japan, photographic portraits began to replace some of these meetings. And, later, Japanese men and women were "introduced" to one another through pictures sent back and forth from Japan and points in the United States or Canada.[1]

On a more general level, people may have a feeling for how Japan and Japanese things are so much a part of a visual culture. Their art forms and even their ways of writing may be given as examples. But beyond that, probably little can be added.

There is an important identification problem here—Japanese and Japanese American are not identical. Stereotypes applied to Japanese culture may have been transferred to Japanese American ethnicity in simplistic and unreflective ways. Historically, this lack of discrimination of things Japanese and Japanese American has caused many personal, social, and political conflicts. Recognition and statements of nationality, ethnic origins, and personal identity continue to be very sensitive and serious issues.

Herein lies one contribution of our study of Japanese American family photography. In the course of our project we have uncovered many facets of a complex relationship of Japanese Americans, personal photography, and ethnic identity. For instance, we will be discussing snapshots taken at the workplace, at funerals, at various farewell occasions that sometimes come into clear and distinct contrast with Anglo American examples. We also find it important to describe what the people in our study did with their personal photographs—from storing them in rubber-banded bundles, to exchanging them through the mail with siblings and other relatives, to making elaborately annotated photo albums. In the course of our interviews and observations, we discovered many things that personal photographs and albums do for people in psychological, social, and cultural ways.

Another facet of our project is easily overlooked. It is amazing in itself that we can find photographs taken by Japanese Americans before the infamous Pearl Harbor incident of December 7, 1941, and years immediately following the internment period. This is especially true regarding photographs that show anything of life before leaving Japan for North America. In Alexander Leighton's book entitled *The Governing of Men*, we find a comment made by a college sophomore after Pearl Harbor and before internment:

> *Now come rumors that the FBI would ransack houses. Everyone becomes frantic. I think every family must have gone through their houses*

in search of indiscriminating articles. Of course most of the items were harmless, yet the FBI agents had a funny way of interpreting innocent articles. We must have burned 50 or 75 books, merely because they were written in Japanese. I spied my mother with tears burning pictures of her relatives back in Japan, looking at them one by one for the last time and burning them *(1946: 32—emphasis added).*

In an historical account found in Elaine Kim's book, *Asian American Literature,* she notes:

> *. . . on the eve of evacuation, many Japanese Americans burned their kimonos, diaries, Japanese language books, letters, photographs, and even their phonograph records and magazines in a panicked effort to destroy whatever might be construed as evidence of their links to Japan in the minds of their oppressors (1982: 134).*

However, we learned that many photographs did survive these disgraceful adverse conditions. Some pictures were hidden or otherwise stored in Japanese churches, Japanese schools, community buildings, or houses that were boarded up during the internment period. Some photographs were packed in the one piece of luggage each internee was allowed to carry to the concentration camps (personal communication, Mary Tayenaka, Dean Yabuki, 1988). We begin to suspect that taking and possessing photographs of one's own family may not always be understood as innocent acts. Indeed these images can be meaningful in different ways, to different people, living in different sociopolitical circumstances.

In addition to the loss of photographs, cameras were confiscated from Japanese American citizens before internment (see Figure 1). In *Desert Exile,* author Yoshiko Uchida writes:

> *Radios with short wave, cameras, binoculars, and firearms were designated as "contraband" and had to be turned in to the police. Obediently adhering to all regulations, we even brought our box cameras to the Berkeley police station where they remained for the duration of the war (1982: 58).*

Figure 1. This piece of family memorabilia appeared in the album of Toy Kenegai. The photograph shows Toy's brother turning in his camera at the Hollenbeck Jail located in Boyle Heights, Los Angeles. This clipping from the Los Angeles Times is dated December 8, 1941, the day after the bombing of Pearl Harbor. The caption notes that all "enemy aliens" on the Pacific Coast were required to surrender their cameras and radios. The newspaper failed to note that Japanese Americans were U.S. citizens, not "aliens." Courtesy of Toy Kenegai.

Clearly there were both external pressures and internal motivations to eliminate pictorial records of the past and prevent photographic recording during the camp years.

Conditions slowly changed during the internment period. At the Topaz camp, for instance, no cameras were allowed initially. But photographs could be taken by people visiting the camp. Japanese American soldiers returning to camp also brought in cameras and took pictures. As in other camps, a photograph studio was established to facilitate the making of family portraits (personal communication, Daisy Satoda, 1989).[2] In other camps, authorized military and civilian personnel were allowed to take photographs. Some pictures did survive these traumatic times, and it was not long before Japanese Americans were using their own cameras once again, even inside the camps.

Two additional points deserve mention here. We see projects like this as an attempt to understand better why people from all over the world have been noticed to treasure their family photographs above and beyond other pieces of their personal material culture. In Philadelphia, for instance, I have noticed that members of contemporary immigrant groups, such as Koreans, Cambodians, Laotians, Vietnamese, and other southeast Asians, seem to arrive with a small collection of their photographs and almost nothing else. Why is this so? We want to develop a more satisfying explanation for why families mourn the loss of their family albums and shoeboxes of portraits and snapshots after a fire has demolished their homes. Or, why, after a wallet is stolen or lost, its owner will claim: "It's not the money so much. Sure I'm worried about someone else using my credit cards. But what will I ever do about my photos? They're gone forever." The survival of photographs and the retention, continuity, or transformation of ethnic and cultural values are themes that run through this book.

The following chapters have been developed in conjunction with a traveling museum exhibition entitled *Turning Leaves: The Photograph Albums of Two Japanese American Families*. That exhibition examined the content, structure, and uses of the photographic collections belonging to two Japanese American families living in different parts of the United States. We sought to understand better the immense popularity of these pictorial forms. We studied personal pictures, first, for their implicit and explicit communicative values and functions, and, second, for their ethnic and cultural significance. We have asked such questions as: What are family photographs intended to communicate? What does one generation want to "say" about itself to other later generations? We have asked how these images complement written and spoken stories—family stories that get repeated on a regular basis and ones that become more valuable as time passes. How do these photographs function as part of the family heritage that is passed on from one generation to the next?

The general themes of this work might seem straightforward and simple at first glance. However, as is so common to outward appearances, much more was revealed when we began to look under the surface. We learned that any discussion of how indigenous representation of ethnic identity can change over time is immensely complex. We found ourselves surrounded by problematic concepts and processes, namely culture change (especially acculturation), representation, ethnicity, and identity. Each of these notions has received generous attention in the academic literature. Even the cultural significance of new abilities to represent oneself through photographic media is currently a topic of concern and debate. We do not pretend to have worked out an original reformulation of how these themes and topics are related to one another. However, the following pages do contain information on what one immigrant group of people has done with these ideas through their seemingly innocent and taken-for-granted acts of taking pictures and making photo albums.

As a modern phenomenon, the personal, social, and cultural aspects of amateur family photography have been taken for granted and rarely studied in depth. In this regard, *Turning Leaves* was quite an unusual project. But our studies do not represent any kind of revolutionary or violent departure from questions social scientists have been asking for years. They are simply focusing on "another way of telling" (Berger and Mohr, 1982). Photographs, in some ways, for some people, have replaced the habits of writing daily diaries and personal journals or the telling of myths, legends, or stories—activities that used to be common events in everyone's life before mass media entered every household. The studies of the Nagano and Uyeda/Miyamura families help to illustrate ways that people from different cultures describe themselves through pictorial modes of communication.

And, finally, this book is as much about the results of the Japanese American Family Album Project as it is about how readers may want to organize and undertake similar studies and projects with other groups of people. We have focused on a topic that everyone can relate to in personal ways based on familiar experience. People from all societies, ethnic groups, cultures, and regions of the world are making and saving photographs of themselves. Rather than having little to say, almost all people are enthusiastic about their pictures and are more than willing to make some comparative comments or observations. Details on this process are found throughout the book. We hope that readers will be inspired to explore the significance of family album imagery in their own lives and in a variety of other contexts.

Chapter One

Family Photograph Collections and the Representation of Ethnicity

The Issei had a great propensity for taking formal photographs to commemorate occasions ranging from birthdays and organizational get-togethers to weddings and even funerals. I suppose this was the only way they could share the event with their families and friends in Japan, but it also resulted in many bulging albums in our households. We had family portraits of all our relatives, most of my parents' friends and their families, and snapshots of every visitor who ever came to our house.[1]

We began our study believing that family photography contained more information than most people realized. We knew that these forms of personal representation were ubiquitous and seemingly taken for granted. Yet everyone told us that these pictures were very important parts of their lives, to be saved, protected, and cherished. Our examination of Japanese American family photography has considered personal pictures as symbolic forms—as the visual products of a process of interpersonal communication. This process is structured by cultural factors and by personal needs to create statements about individual and social existence. Throughout the study we sought to understand better the details of both real life accomplishments and photographic activities performed by members of one ethnic group—a group that had undergone considerable social and cultural change over three generations. We wanted to know more about what two families of Japanese Americans were saying about themselves through their own pictures—their own means of pictorial representation.

While preparing for this study, we learned that questions about culture, communication, identity, ethnicity, continuity, and change have seldom been combined and applied to forms of personal photography. What started as a straightforward attempt to understand and honor people who take the time and effort to keep photographic accounts of family life developed into a much more complicated project. It became apparent that we needed to examine the broad dimensions of photographic representation and pictorial communication, in general, and family photography in particular. In short, we needed to know much more about the historical and cultural significances of family photography, its variety, and uses as a medium of personal communication.

Situating Family Photography as a Topic of Study

Personal photography and family albums have received uneven attention within the social sciences and the humanities. With a few exceptions—noted at points in this book—sociologists, historians, anthropologists, psychologists, folklorists, and communication scholars have refrained from taking sustained and serious looks at amateur forms of photography. In some cases, historians have paid primary attention to progressions of technological developments and innovations; in others, authors have attended to aesthetic features, comparing professional and nonprofessional forms of photography. In yet others, observers have concentrated on the psychological characteristics of snapshots and related amateur forms. But relatively little attention has been given to how these vernacular forms present and re-present life in pictorial form—as culturally structured representation. We find a similar neglect of seeing how ordinary people create narratives from sequences of these images found in album form. Few professional observers have attempted a coordinated view of relationships among picturetakers, their photograph albums, and the ways family members look at, use, exhibit, and revere their picture collections. The Japanese American Family Album Project represented an attempt to reverse this trend and to demonstrate what can be learned from applying a perspective sensitive both to cultural issues and communication concerns.

Historically, the family album frequently occupied a significant and revered place within the family's domestic setting. Its prominence is demonstrated by the fact that people used to display it next to the family Bible. Robert Taft, author of *Photography and the American Scene,* writes that for families on the frontier in the 1860s,

> *home was finally complete when the Bible and the album could be brought out from the trunks and placed in the center of the room. The Bible was the consolation of these wayfarers from a far country; the album was the most direct tie to their past life, for it contained the images of those most loved and now far distant: Father—Mother— Aunt Sue—Sister Mary, and a host of others (1938: 138).*

In this way, family genealogies were documented and preserved in leather-bound editions, complete with gold hinges and clasps, sometimes covered with velvet and lace. At first, albums were filled with studio portraits; collections of 2½-by-4-inch carte-de-visite studio-made photographs, along with larger portrait images, were very popular. The locations of these pictures were limited to settings constructed from theatrical backdrops and accompanying props.

After 1888, however, popular use of cameras was liberated from the confines of the professional studio. George Eastman introduced the now famous "You Press the Button, and We Do the Rest" practice of photography. Historian Beaumont Newhall notes that Eastman called the Kodak a photographic notebook that "enables the fortunate possessor to go back by the light of his own fireside to scenes which would otherwise fade from memory and be lost" (1982: 129). Cameras were now produced for popular consumption, and professional processing and printing were made available to ordinary people at a reasonable expense. Designed to be portable, these new, easy-to-use cameras were reduced in size and weight; lenses and film stock allowed people to record images in a variety of settings previously unknown to studio photographers. In turn, photograph albums began to illustrate a greater freedom of choice for where and when people preferred to take pictures. Ordinary people could now show how they wanted *themselves* to appear; people were gaining more choices and increased control over their own representations.

However, cameras were not made available to all groups of people across the world, and all groups of people did not begin to make their own personal photographs in identical ways. For instance, many people continued to rely on visits to neighborhood photographers or use the services of itinerant photographers. From his observations of Asian American albums, anthropologist Malcolm Collier has noticed that personal photographs from China or the Philippines prior to World War II are almost always professionally produced images, some from studio settings, others not so. But personal photographs made in nonprofessional contexts from Japan and Asian American sources in the United States seem to appear earlier (personal communication, 1988). The fact that Meiji-era Japan eagerly embraced photography may be related to this finding.[2]

In retrospect, we must now acknowledge that nonprofessional forms of photography have become the most common and popular forms of picture-making in the world. According to the annually published *Wolfman Report on the Photographic Industry,* over *14.9 billion* still pictures were made by amateur photographers in the United States alone in 1987.[3] The same report also indicates that approximately 95 percent of U.S. households contain at least one camera. By whatever measure one wishes to use, we are clearly the most pictured people in the history of the human condition.

Given all this photographic activity, it is equally significant that so little is critically written about home photography when compared to the attention given to fine art photography, photojournalism, and forms of commercial photography. Our current interest, however, is less with quantity of picture-making than with a qualitative evaluation of a family's photograph collection. We have examined what two Japanese American families were doing with their cameras and photographs as part of personal communication and shared culture. In this sense, our study attempted to stimulate new forms of attention to relationships of ordinary people, everyday life, and leisure time photographic activities.

Studying Family Photography as Social Communication

One orienting principle of our study was that family photography is primarily a medium of communication. We felt that if we approached snapshots and family albums from this perspective, new and important relationships about personal reports, identity, and ethnicity would emerge.

Elsewhere I have described the "home-mode of visual/pictorial communication" as one way of analyzing the pictorial products and social process of amateur photography (Chalfen 1987). I outlined the structural and functional dimensions of home-mode communication, and I compared home-modes with mass modes of public communication. In this model I am more concerned with a social process of human communication than I am with uses of specific pieces of camera equipment (still, motion picture, or video) or with the professional or "amateur" status of the photographer.[4] In home-mode activity, snapshots, family movies, and home videotapes are all examples of interpersonal and small group communication—instances of ordinary people making pictorial statements about themselves to and for themselves and succeeding generations of family members.

This general perspective has guided much of our research on the photographs made and kept by the Japanese American families in our study. Initially we asked questions about picture content. Which people are regularly seen and shown in their photographs? What topics and themes appear on a regular basis? In terms of process, which family members were responsible for taking pictures or for organizing the collection into boxes, albums, or wall displays? In addition, how did members of these Japanese American families use their pictures? For instance, who decided that certain photographs should be duplicated and possibly mailed to relatives and friends? What did they expect other people to do with them? What are some of the psychological and social functions associated with this kind of personal photography? In short, we wanted to understand the composition and topography of the world shown in Japanese American personal photographs, the factors that structured this view of life, and what members of these Japanese American families did with it.

These questions make it very clear that many choices and decisions are involved in this process of communication. Most people are not aware of all the choices that are available; they may be even less aware that they have made many decisions along the way. Some of these decisions can be stated as explicitly intentional; others are more implicitly realized and appear to be just taken for granted. Many choices and decisions become internalized, and result in culturally accepted and generally unquestioned conventions of representation. Our analysis has attempted to clarify the conscious and unconscious decisions that form the process of making family photographs and organizing photograph collections.

Intentions, Choices, and Decisions in Family Photography

Photographer and anthropologist Paul Byers reminds us that cameras don't take pictures—people do (1966).[5] But what do "people do" with their cameras? And how has this potential freedom of choice been exercised at different historical times and in different parts of the world? The historical development of camera technology and sensitive film stocks seems to allow for the photography of anything—that is, anyone can take a picture of anything at any time for any reason. Technology allows it; advertisements promote it; scientists exploit it. But do, in fact, ordinary people from all parts of the world "take advantage" of this potential? Do snapshot collections or family albums demonstrate this freedom of choice? Do the photographic results of amateur camera use illustrate schemes of random-like behavior? Or can we find patterns of choices—is it the case that only certain people take certain kinds of pictures of certain people, places, events, activities? If the latter is observed more frequently than the former, what is "controlling" or even "determining" the patterned selection of content for snapshots and family albums? In short, many human decisions must be made. But it appears that most people have been culturally conditioned to keep these decisions as unproblematic as possible—they are part of our culture.

Several stages of decision-making are easily discerned in any creation of photographic representation. People are in charge of deciding when to take pictures, where to place the camera, how to hold it, and the exact instant of exposure.[6] Family photographers and their subjects have to decide who or what to include or exclude. In order to produce snapshots, ordinary people make choices and decisions just as artists and commercial photographers do. However snapshooters do this in more informal and less conscious ways; people on both sides of the camera usually agree on "what to do." That is, *both* behavior behind the camera *and* in front of the camera conforms to conventions of this representative subgenre—each person playing a role and taking responsibility for "doing it right." Before rolls of snapshots go to the drugstore or photo shop for processing and printing, several levels of decision-making have already taken place (see Figure 2).

These decisions and choices may differ from one group of people to another. However, at the moment, we know very little about how these decisions have been historically or culturally organized, or, for that matter, distinguished from one another. Social scientists have recognized that different cultures celebrate different stages of life history in different manners. These differences may influence the ways people decide to structure a pictorial or photographic memory of their lives. For instance, societies may differ with regard to allowing, promoting, or prohibiting photography of specific celebrations or ritualistic activities, and to making photographs on different days in relation to the birth or death of family members (or of dead children or adults). Cultural differences may also play a role in determining which events are too personal for photographic recording, who should or should not be photographed, where and/or when certain photographs should or should not be displayed, or even, who should or should not see certain pictures at a later time.[7] For instance, we asked if the Japanese

Figure 2. A cartoon by Pete Hironaka as it appeared in the *Pacific Citizen* on June 25, 1982. This newspaper is published by the Japanese American Citizens League (JACL) and is widely distributed throughout the United States. Personal thanks to Don Rundstrom for calling it to my attention.

American examples in our study provided any special combination of topics or themes that were seldom or never seen in Anglo American photograph albums.

Organizing a family album represents a second major stage of decision-making. It is also one of the ways that snapshots may be used as a personal medium of communication after the pictures are developed. Although some snapshots will be tucked away in envelopes or stored in shoeboxes, other photographs seem to get special attention. Specific pictures may be duplicated and mailed to relatives and friends; others may be enlarged and framed for placement on household furniture or walls. Others may be duplicated or cut to fit into wallets, lockets, or photo cubes. The most popular and ambitious alternative has been to organize pictures into photograph albums.

We also recognize that people organize their pictures in different ways, sometimes making different types of photograph albums.[8] In doing so, they must make many other kinds of decisions—the themes, topics, and content may differ from album to album. The creation of a family album usually requires considerable attention to problems of organization, placement, sequence, captioning, juxtaposition. Sometimes people will simply put every picture they have into the same album or sequence of albums, and this collection becomes known as the Family Album. The Family Album may be started shortly after a couple is married, and, as such, is organized to celebrate their lives together. But their total photograph collection is quickly enlarged. The couple may have brought individual albums into the marriage. And separate albums such as Baby Albums may have been made to document the birth and growth of each child in the family.[9]

Other extensions of the category of Family Album are found in photograph albums devoted to specific topics, places, or events. Family members may devote an entire album to their trip to Hawaii or Cape Cod, or to their European summer tour. In addition to the Travel Album, we also find examples of the Vacation Album, focused on "Our Summer at the Shore" or "Our Week at Disneyland." Or, a significant religious event may become the central topic of attention—Confirmation Albums, Baptism Albums, Bar or Bat Mitzvah Albums are a few examples. Special family events may receive (or seemingly demand) photographic attention, as in the ubiquitous Wedding Album (as well as Honeymoon Albums), Birthday Albums, Prom Albums, or Family Reunion Albums. In other cases, people feel comfortable making Pet Albums, War Albums or, in rarer cases, Funeral Albums.[10]

We should recognize that not everyone is inclined to create a family album. A family member may simply feel a need to "bring some order to all those pictures that are just lying around in drawers or boxes." In some cases, social factors or life circumstances may subtly promote this activity. One example is provided by the stage in life that social scientists call "life review." An individual may attempt to order the past as an aid to understanding the present. One member of the Gallup Japanese American family, Chiko Miyamura Herrera, told us:

> *It is a moment in time. I just enjoy taking pictures. I can say that, and of course when you're young, you don't think of it that way. After you get older, you'll find out that you enjoy it more looking back on those pictures or you'll remember at times when you took those pictures. Like the kids when they go to the prom now, and they take a picture, and, maybe, now it doesn't mean much to them but say forty years from now . . . then they'll remember: "Oh yeah, I remember that girl I took out to the prom. . . ." They'll start thinking about the good time they had or whatever. And, I think pictures do that to a person to make you remember the good times.*

In previous studies, family members have confessed a sense of guilt about their procrastination: "We never seem to get around to putting them all together—they're in envelopes and boxes and drawers all over the house. But someday I'll organize them and that will be nice." I have also heard: "I hope one of our children will think of doing that for us!" However it is safe to claim that nearly all families have a collection of personal photographs in one form or another. This generalization seems to be true even for people living in the most remote regions of the world, where personal camera ownership is rare. Throughout the world the personal photograph is a very well-distributed artifact.

In summary, we are emphasizing that the existence of family albums and photograph collections in general represents the products of many human decisions. Camera manufacturers regularly supply directions for the mechanical use of their products. These directions imply patterns of cultural behavior. For instance, they may advocate "correct" choices of subject matter, locations, and settings for photography as well as a preferred way of looking at people, places, events, and objects. But ultimately these choices must be made by ordinary people as they use their camera equipment in personal contexts. For instance, in one study of contemporary Japanese family photography, we read:

> *It is typical for a young Japanese family to take hundreds of pictures*

of their home and children before the children are two years of age.
In addition they are likely to include many pictures of the husband at
work in their collection. Family pictures include everyday activities
which would be considered inappropriate by American standards, such
as diapering babies, breastfeeding, family members bathing together,
family members sleeping together, preparing food and feeding babies
and young children (Blinn 1986: 12).[11]

We may even want to ask if different social groups have unconsciously developed or overtly recognized an etiquette surrounding their camera and picture-using behaviors.[12]

The significance of photograph collections in this study, however, comes from Japanese Americans, their ideas and norms for appropriate behavior as they take and use pictures as part of everyday life and cultural circumstances, and from our interpretations of what they were doing. Rather than accepting such cliched and misleading phrases as "pictures speak for themselves" or that "a picture is worth a thousand words," we set out to learn what specific people have to say about their personal pictures and *which* thousand words were most relevant to the relationship between their lives and their photographs. Rather than thinking of the images in our project as the results of camera technology, we are exploring the structure and functions of these pictures as products of Japanese, Japanese American, and American cultures.

Family Photography as the Construction of Communicative
Statements and Interpretations of Life

A communications approach leads us to ask who is saying what to whom under what personal, social, and cultural circumstances for what reasons and with what expected and unanticipated results and effects? With specific attention to home-mode communication, we are prompted to consider family photographs as context-bound "statements" rather than as just pictures, souvenirs, or "copies of life." Borrowing from the thinking of Gregory Bateson, any symbolic form, including a photograph, may be regarded as both a report and an interpretive statement. And, as Roland Barthes has reiterated in his book *Camera Lucida,* photographs "report" by communicating the message, "that-has-been" (1981: 77). People generally accept the referential functions of photographic imagery, but interpretive characteristics of photographs are more elusive and more controversial.

In our study, photograph collections in general, and family albums in particular, are being treated as statements—such as accounts, reports, and pictorial versions or renditions of life. Each one of these terms deserves additional qualification and critical assessment. For instance, personal, social, or cultural statement? Statements and reports directed to whom? A rendition of all of life? Statements similar to biographical or autobiographical accounts? Version of life as in a life history?

This treatment of family photographs as social statements is similar to what historian Alan Thomas suggests in his observations of Victorian family albums:

> *A Victorian family's photography album can be personally and socially revealing to a degree at first little appreciated when the leather covers fall back to expose those distant reticent faces. . . . [C]areful repeated reading and the discovery of the facts of ownership (frequently a simple matter) transform the situation: the album becomes a living social document, richer in its appeal to the imagination . . . and unique in its concrete, visual record of worlds of past experience. . . . [A]nd because the images we see are actual, located in time, space and social class, a sense of that particular world—a social statement, in short—also emerges (1977: 43).*

The existence of pictorial versions of life has been generally ignored in the literature on biography and autobiography (Langness and Frank 1981). Attention has remained with written and spoken forms, and only passing or tangential consideration has been given to the fact that far more people make and keep photographic accounts of their lives than written ones. With noted exceptions, the comparative existence and organization of these ubiquitous materials have escaped most observers.

Making individual snapshots and combining them into photograph albums can be aligned with what has been referred to as "autobiographical distortions"—although this term seems to imply that there is one "right" or "correct" way and others are merely imperfect variations or distortions of the more accurate version. But "correct" or "accurate" to whom? Perhaps an acknowledgment of multiple autobiographical constructions would be more appropriate. If one accepts the simultaneous existence of multiple views, then one must direct attention toward an analysis of the variations, the similarities, and differences across several views. Collections of snapshots and personal photographs in general can be understood as interpretations in their own right. These perceptions and interpretations are sometimes accompanied by written and/or spoken annotations, sometimes not. We shall see that albums in our study made by George Nagano illustrate the former while those made by Frank Uyeda illustrate the latter. In either case, we are faced with the problem of interpreting these interpretations (Geertz 1973) from records that are primarily visual and pictorial.

What, then, were the Japanese American families in this project saying about themselves? What observations and statements were being expressed in this medium of communication? Which individuals or groups of people were being addressed in either formal or informal ways? These questions became central to our methods of study and analysis.

Relationships of Family Photographs and Ethnic Identity

Another premise in our communications approach to family photography implies that pictures are understood as symbolic forms—forms that comprise the many mediums of communicative interaction that humans, by virtue of being human, have with their environment. Humans relate to their natural and cultural environments almost entirely through the use of symbols, arbitrarily created and interpreted according to culturally derived systems of conventions and patterns of meanings. Here we find logical connections between symbolic components of culture and photographic communication. We find one example of such a connection in the introduction to Kiefer's study of culture change and the Japanese American community:

> *The arbitrariness and elasticity of symbols is both an asset and a liability to man the symbolizer.* His symbols allow him to play creatively with his environment, but they also make it very hard for him to feel absolutely certain about the stability and orderliness of that environment. *Mutual agreement among men about the "real" order of the environment is therefore a great help to every man's sanity. Culture, as a shared symbol system, can be understood partly as a defense against the sort of perceptual disintegration whose possibility is so poignantly illustrated by [James] Joyce. Partly for this reason, men defend their culture vigorously against alien ways of seeing the world* (1974: xv–xvi, emphasis added).

Making family photographs and organizing albums are modern additions to a human's many ways of symbolically defining and ordering the world. This can also be understood as an attempt to satisfy needs to settle on a way that things are, and to make statements about the real order of the environment. This is, in fact, a mode of symbolic manipulation.

Sociologist Erving Goffman confirms this perspective in another way and helps us understand better the internal consistency of human symbolic behavior:

> *What people understand to be the organization of their experience, they buttress, and perforce, self-fulfillingly. They develop a corpus of cautionary tales, games, riddles, experiments, newsy stories, and other scenarios, which elegantly confirm a frame-relevant view of the world. . . . And the human nature that fits with this view of viewings does so in part because its possessors have learned to comport themselves so as to render this analysis true to them. Indeed, in countless ways and ceaselessly, social life takes up and freezes into itself the understandings we have of it* (1974: 563).

We are suggesting that family photographs, and especially photograph albums, can be added to this inventory of "newsy stories, and other scenarios, which elegantly confirm a frame-relevant view of the world." And rather than promoting a sense of disintegration, photograph albums seem to offer a sense of integration of bits and pieces of the world into a satisfactory, mentally soothing, stabilizing, and/or peaceful way. James Kaufmann, an American Studies scholar, has stated: "the ritual making of family photographs—like most strategies for ordering experience— . . . offer[s] soothing evidence that our lives are better and sometimes more coherent than we sometimes believe" (1980: 244). And so, we lay the groundwork for integrating themes of coherence, defining experience, and even storytelling as expressed in family photographs made by Japanese Americans.

In turn, this understanding of photographic representation as symbolic behavior provides a logical connection to questions of identity in general and ethnicity in particular. Concepts of ethnicity, ethnic group, and ethnic identity have played fundamental roles in our project. The scholarly literature indicates that each one of these concepts is problematic and is often not given sufficient theoretical attention. We have attempted to interpret what family album photography can say about ethnicity by asking how people produce their own statements of ethnic identity through the family album as a medium of communication.

Relationships between ethnicity, cultural symbols, and symbolic behavior are found in the writings of anthropologists Ronald Reminick and George De Vos:

> *The cultural symbols of ethnicity provide the members with a feeling of continuity, belonging, familiarity, commitment, and reciprocal obligations which perpetuate the general aims and ideals of the group. For the individual, ethnicity provides a context for affective expressiveness of one's distinctive ethnic culture and identity, attenuates the experience of relative deprivation (or heightens it if the goals and expectations have not been fully met), and provides a social security system for those members who make up that group (Reminick 1983: 60, emphasis added).*

When George De Vos examines the significance and influence of such factors as racial uniqueness, economic bases, religion, aesthetic cultural patterns, and language on ethnic identity, he concludes:

> *the ethnic identity of a group of people consists of their subjective symbolic or emblematic use* of any aspect of culture, *in order to differentiate themselves from other groups. These emblems can be imposed from outside or embraced from within. Ethnic features such as language or clothing or food can be considered emblems, for they show others who one is and to what group one belongs. . . . As a subjective sense of belonging, ethnicity cannot be defined by behavioral criteria alone. Ethnicity is determined by what a person feels about himself, not by how he is observed to behave. Defining oneself in social terms is one basic answer to* the human need to belong *and to survive (1975: 16–17, emphasis added).*

De Vos argues that the endurance of ethnic or cultural identity has been neglected as a primary social force—important as nationalism or social class affiliation. He stresses that a psychocultural approach to social belonging is fundamental to understanding social behavior (1975: 7, 38). Our point is that photography can also be understood as social behavior. We have focused on how Japanese Americans made "subjective symbolic or emblematic use" of part of their material culture, namely the taking, organizing, and sharing of their personal photographs. In Chapter Five we will discuss how the notion of belonging seems to tie together several of these thematic concerns.

Issues of Cultural Continuity and Change

Questions of social and culture change became central to our attempts to relate culture and ethnic identity to family photography. The Japanese Americans in our study had undergone and witnessed a tremendous number of changes in their lives. In turn, they were asking their children to understand these changes in certain ways. We were interested in learning how these people were using their photograph collections to sift, select, discard, and retrieve specific points in and about their lives for commemoration in the form of a pictorial memory. From this perspective—and contrary to some of our initial thinking—we began to view continuity as something more special than change. That is, we feel that change must be understood as the norm, and that continuity is to be studied as an extraordinary and problematic phenomenon.

In general, questions of continuity and change are extremely complex. One may be mistaken for the other without proper reference to behavioral context. Continuity and discontinuity can take place at the same time; insistence on specifying one or the other may be an inappropriate imposition of a cultural need for dualisms and/or polar opposites. Notions of transformation and reformulation of cultural values, for instance, may suggest a parallel expression of continuity and change (Malcolm Collier, personal communication, 1988). The celebration of special birthday parties by the Nagano family, as described in Chapter Five, will provide an interesting example. In addition, relying on photographic or mechanically produced versions of these expressions may further complicate the analysis.

In working through the expression of continuity and change, we found some interesting ties to how we were thinking about ethnicity. Drawing once again on the work of George De Vos:

> *Ethnicity, therefore, is in its narrowest sense a feeling of continuity with the past, a feeling that is maintained as an essential part of one's self-definition. Ethnicity is also intimately related to the individual need for collective continuity. . . . Ethnicity, therefore, includes a sense of personal survival in the historical continuity of the group (1975: 17).*

Previous mention of symbolic components and manifestations of culture becomes relevant once again. De Vos goes on to say that in some ways, progenitors and parents continue to "live" as long "as some symbols of their culture are carried forth into the present and future out of the past. Ethnicity in its deepest psychological level is a sense of survival" (1975: 17). This, in turn, raises questions about the roles that photographic materials, as symbolic forms, play in this process of continuity, change, and transformation in Japanese American culture.

In summary we have been interested in finding pictorial evidence of how the Japanese Americans in our study showed themselves in a process of change. It seemed natural to begin by studying how snapshots could be understood as a way of tracking history and change as seen from the inside—by participants themselves. We slowly realized that maybe change was not as important an issue as finding examples of continuity—how certain elements, traits, values, patterns of behavior have persisted in the face of all that has happened to generations of these families. It then became a more sophisticated task to learn how combinations and patterns of both continuity and change were expressed in this mode of pictorial communication.

Theoretical Orientations

The juxtaposition of these theoretical points and perspectives with the subject matter of family albums has generated several kinds of logical expectations and speculative explanations. In general we have been exploring the potential influence of culture, value scheme, generation, and regional affiliation on what people do with their personal photography and the kinds of messages they produce about themselves.

For instance, we have worked on the expectation that cultural differences would make a difference in the content, forms, and use of personal photographs. This kind of expectation is based on such statements as:

> *Particular cultures afford particular patterns related to aesthetic traditions used symbolically as a basis of self and social identity. Tastes in food, dance traditions, styles of clothing, and definitions of physical beauty are all examples of how cultures identify themselves by aesthetic patterns (De Vos 1975: 15).*

Again, personal photography can be added to this list of examples. Culture plays an important role in what people do with their cameras, how they prefer to appear in photographs, and how they organize and use their pictures. In this way of thinking, printed directions that accompany the purchase of new cameras may be less important than the conscious and unconscious directives supplied by the culture of the family photographer. The alternative expectation is that the use of inexpensive, mass produced cameras has created a homogeneity in aesthetic pattern that has eliminated the existence of cultural differences. (See Chapter Six for a discussion of "camera culture.") However, all analyses of this kind must also consider the active relationship or dynamic interplay between pushes and pulls of diversity and homogeneity.

A related series of expectations focuses on the question of cultural values and the problematic relationship of values and photography. One question that seems to stand out in much of the literature on ethnicity and identity involves a comparison of values. For instance, social scientists make a strong case for the predominance of five major Japanese core values (sometimes referred to as "major orientations") of collectivity, duty and obligation, hierarchy, deference, and dependency. Would pictorial manifestations of these core values be reflected in the photograph collections of Japanese Americans? And a parallel question: Would the major American orientations of individualism, equality, a concern for rights and privileges, self-reliance, and self-assertion be reflected in the Japanese American albums? These questions introduce the problematic issues of how one photographs a value, and of recognizing the "visual representation" of particular values in photograph collections.[13]

With questions of comparative values, we are logically led to include another set of expectations based on generational differences of Japanese Americans. For instance, would it be more logical to expect the Japanese values to wane, become less prominent, or even disappear in the photographs made and collected by succeeding generations of Japanese Americans? Being consistent, could we legitimately expect the core American values to become more obvious, manifest, and distinct in succeeding generations?[14] Or does this type of question impose too much of a linear orientation—one that might preclude the emergence of a separate and distinct pattern of Japanese American ethnicity?

The Japanese are the only ethnic group in America who specify each of their generations from the original immigrant group with a distinct linguistic term. The term *Issei* refers to first generation immigrants from Japan; Nisei are second generation, or children of Issei; Sansei are third generation, or children of Nisei; and Yonsei are fourth generation, or children of Sansei. According to some authors, each of these generations is accorded a profile of unique personality characteristics. As summarized by Stanford Lyman:

> *Moreover, from the standpoint of any single moving generational group, the others are imputed to have peculiar and distinctive personalities and attendant behavior patterns which are evaluated in positive and negative terms. Each generation removed from Japan is assumed to have its own characterological qualities, qualities which are derived at the outset from its spacio-temporal position, and are thus not subject to voluntaristic adoption or obviation. Thus, each generation is living out a unique, temporally governed lifetime which shall not be seen again after it is gone (1970: 83).*

This kind of theorizing led another scholar to consider how generational difference and "personal interpretations" of history affected his results in a study of Japanese Americans living in San Francisco: "When I began the analysis of historical perceptions, I expected to find clear-cut perceptual styles peculiar to each generation—issei, nisei, and sansei" (Kiefer 1974: 54–55).[15] Kiefer's perspective is directly relevant to our project—namely getting a better hold on which factors (psychological, cultural) are responsible for different generational interpretations of history.

Thus we return to our earlier question: Is it reasonable to expect that some of the unique qualities of each generation of Japanese Americans are preserved in symbolic form in family albums? Can photographs and albums made by members of each generation reflect certain "characterological qualities" associated with each generation, and, in fact, be used to distinguish one generational group from another? If these generations are as distinct as is suggested, this should be possible.[16]

The fourth set of expectations surrounds the issue of regional differences. Clearly not all members of the same immigrant group settle in the same geographic area. While there may be a clumping pattern during the early stages of immigration, as time passes, people change their residences, for employment opportunities or to escape discrimination, or for other reasons. Christie Kiefer found: "The San Francisco Japanese American community is distinguished from the non-Japanese population of San Francisco on the bases of *intensity, generality,* and *history,* and it is distinguished from the Japanese American communities outside San Francisco on the bases of *intensity, history,* and *geography*" (1974: 7). With specific attention to identity, Kiefer adds:

> *different sociocultural milieux present very different problems and resources in the person struggling to maintain a workable identity and that consequently very different strategies may be called for in different societies at different stages. Identity maintenance is crucially affected by the number, variety, size, power, accessibility, moral rigidity, homogeneity, and permanence of reference groups in a person's milieu—as well as the changes in all these factors over the life cycle—and by the moral content of the meaning system and roles that are important to him (1974: 232–33).*

Some of this thinking contributed to the significance of selecting Japanese American families from two different geographic locations of the United States. We learned that historical circumstances surrounding any process of immigration can be deceiving and complex. There is usually considerable overlap between historic and geographic variables; as such they are neither mutually exclusive or exhaustive. Complexities arise when different members of the same generation, including siblings, move to different regions of the country. For instance, in the Uyeda/ Miyamura family, more than the Nagano family, we shall see that regional differences can influence generational behaviors in significant ways. Different perspectives on life, or, specifically, on the immigration experience may result from very different patterns of acculturation and diverse collections of influences. Thus we developed other questions that addressed the potential reflection and expression of these alternative experiences in their photograph collections.

Limitations of the Research Design and Our Results

What initially might appear as a fairly straightforward examination of a few photograph collections develops into a dense mesh of dependent and independent variables. The orienting principle that regularly appears in our research—that photographs must be understood as symbolic forms, as cultural artifacts, and as a medium of communication—produces a theoretical complexity that can be easily overlooked. In turn, the results and findings are dependent on the variety and depth of questions being asked. But it is highly unlikely that any one project could address all levels and layers of this complexity. We have not provided satisfactory explanations for all the theoretical expectations outlined in previous pages; many questions remain to be addressed in other projects. Not all these questions are answered by this study. They are included here to give some feeling for how a set of deceivingly simple questions can produce a complicated and far-reaching pattern of inquiry.

In this sense, it is important to recognize several kinds of limitations of our work as we reveal the project's results. For instance, we have made a determined effort to examine collections of photographs from two separate Japanese American families. Our results come from two case studies rather than a statistically derived sample of Japanese American families and their photograph collections. (See Appendix A for additional comment.) We have not focused our attention on individual pictures mainly because we have been looking for patterns of both image content and photographic habits. Nor have we tried to make definitive statements about the characteristics that would make a specific snapshot identifiable as Japanese American. Our examination has been limited to what two families have habitually done with home-mode photography as a social process and symbolic activity.

While we have suggested important relationships between cultural values and family photographs, it is important to remember two points that have continued to play a significant role in our analysis. First, album pictures do not offer information on all cultural values. Secondly, we are studying the interaction of cultural values and camera-using values. Camera use is surrounded by societal norms and values about what is appropriate for photographic content and display (Chalfen 1987). Does camera use in home-mode communication seem to ignore and bypass such variables as cultural values, generational differences, regional affiliation, or even the introduction of new kinds of recording technologies? Does the use of cameras and pictures in the home-mode create a homogeneous pattern of representation?[17] We are looking to see how "Kodak culture" and immigrant ethnic cultural values—associated with Japanese Americans—overlap and intersect with one another.

Chapter Two

The Selection of
Two Japanese American Families

Methods of Working with Families and their Photographs

Our methods of family selection, fieldwork, and analysis drew upon previous research in two major areas: indigenous or "native-generated" photography and filmmaking, as well as studies of Japanese and Japanese American culture.

Within the study of personal photography, two models of research dominate the literature on native-generated imagery. In the first model, members of a particular community are actually asked to make photographs, a film, or a videotape, often for the first time. They are instructed in the basic technology of image production, but not in choice of content or aesthetics. Their pictures and their picture-making behaviors become the focus of study. Research questions usually involve relationships between image content and cultural characteristics of the people who made them. This paradigm includes research on film communication directed by Sol Worth and John Adair with Navajo Indians (1972), by Beryl Bellman and Bennetta Jules-Rosette in East and Central Africa (1977), by myself with teenagers living in Philadelphia (1981), among several others.

The other model is characterized by less coerced examples of image making: that is, when the still photographs or motion pictures already exist before curious research personnel arrive on the scene. In these cases, the pictures were made as part of "natural" behavior, on personal initiatives, and as part of everyday life. Examples following this model of research include my own studies of home-mode communication (1988, 1987, 1984), as well as those by Christopher Musello (1980), Karin Ohrn (1975), Lynn Blinn (1986), Michael Lesy (1980), Julia Hirsch (1981), and a small but growing collection of international studies. However, not all of this literature has been useful. Methods and objectives differ from study to study. The main limitation for our purposes is that very few authors have been explicit about how their examples of personal photography can be understood as a culturally structured form of communication. The development of this theme is central to our examination of Japanese American family photography.

We realized that our findings about family photography would be meaningless unless we developed our interpretations in contexts of culture and communication. How did our observations on camera and photograph use fit into other culturally structured habits and patterns of life? We interpreted our observations in light of independent findings reported in academic and popular literature on Japanese and Japanese American culture. We did not seek to initiate an independent study of Japanese American values; nor did we attempt to take a random sampling of Japanese American communities. Our review of the literature on this topic revealed that several comprehensive studies had already been done and proved to be adequate for our interpretive needs. Here I refer to work on Japanese American culture by Evelyn N. Glenn (1986), Sylvia J. Yanagisako (1985), Akemi Kikumura (1981), John Modell (1977), John W. Connor (1977), Christie W. Kiefer (1974), William Peterson (1971), and Harry H. L. Kitano (1969) as well as work by Robert J. Smith (1983, 1978, 1974), Takie S. Lebra (1976), Chie Nakane (1970), among others on Japanese culture. We were disappointed to learn that with the exception of Smith's writing and references to picture brides, personal uses of photographs are virtually never mentioned in these sources.

Developing Two Case Studies

We decided to base our studies of Japanese American personal photography on original fieldwork using case study methods of observation, description, and analysis.[1] The case-study approach is preferred when researchers are exploring new areas, and when one objective is to generate as much qualitative data as possible. We were not able to make reliable and systematic comparisons with a large number of previous studies. An established and tested program of field methodology did not exist for the kinds of questions we were asking about home-mode communication in a cross-cultural frame of reference. Since this project was breaking new ground, we had to take certain chances with our methods and means of study, but we wanted to be as explicit as possible about who we were choosing and why.

The planning phases of our two case studies focused on locating family members who would be enthusiastic about participating in the project. We also needed to make sure that families had appropriate collections of photographs for the study. A family that professed an intense interest in personal photographs and family biographies but actually had only a few examples of such pictures would not have been as acceptable as a family with a rich and varied collection of materials. The photograph collections belonging to families that responded to our solicitations were screened for the following characteristics:

1. *The quantity and quality of photographs in the family collection. By "quality" we meant materials that were in relatively good condition and were suitable for study, reproduction and possible enlargement, and display (for purposes of museum exhibition).*
2. *Photographic materials that depicted or related to several generations of the same family. We wanted to be able to study forms of cross-generational representation.*
3. *Written materials (journals, diaries) or pictorial records (scrapbooks, artwork) that would facilitate the development of both individual and social histories. We wanted to see how individual, family, and local community histories were related to patterns of occupations, social and religious affiliations, recreational activities, and so on.*
4. *Availability and willingness of family members from different generations to participate in the project, to be interviewed, to show us their photograph collections, and make sure we were using their materials in correct and appropriate ways. Using such personal materials, we wanted to establish a collaborative relationship as much as possible, reducing the sense of people as "research subjects."*

Locating Appropriate Case Study Families

We purposely selected families from two different regions of the country in order to explore the regional adaptations of Japanese Americans to alternative social, geographic, political, and historical circumstances (see "Expectations" in Chapter One). Los Angeles was chosen to represent a large urban community, one with the largest Japanese American population in the United States. In contrast, Gallup, New Mexico was selected as a relatively isolated inland community with a much smaller Japanese American population.[2]

The Los Angeles component of the project was initially generated out of the Japanese American Culture and Community Center (JACCC). The selection of families was facilitated by the collection of resources and contacts from this community organization. We realized that the JACCC was responsible for informing the community of its activities and projects. As such, the selection of families would reflect upon the community, the institution, and its personnel.

Family participation was solicited through notices in bilingual newspapers, Japanese television coverage, brochures, presentations, personal contacts, and letters. The responding families demonstrated an interesting set of characteristics. They expressed a sense of pride in family history and family name. They also were interested in preserving their family photographs as historical documents for the community. In many cases, the albums shown to project staff belonged to a recently deceased member of an Issei family, and the albums were an inheritance. Family members were deciding what they should do with their valued photographs, and, in this sense, they imagined the proposed exhibition as a kind of memorial.

The George Nagano family was selected as the Los Angeles family for participation in the California pilot project and the proposed exhibition for the National Endowment for the Humanities. Nagano family members showed us photograph albums that depicted several generations of relatives and friends. After some initial inspection, we recognized that the Nagano photographic records were closely aligned with the history of the Los Angeles Japanese American community. For instance, important linkages to Japanese American neighborhoods, church and community activities, employment experiences, periods of evacuation, and the postwar resettlement activities were all accounted for in the Nagano materials. George Nagano's family album (described in Chapter Three) was particularly fascinating for its quality and quantity of commentary, photographs, and scrapbook content as well as its elaborate integration of written and pictorial forms.

The New Mexico component of the project was initially organized as a parallel project sponsored by the Maxwell Museum of Anthropology at the University of New Mexico in Albuquerque. The pilot project was funded by the New Mexico Humanities Council with some additional support from an NEH Planning Grant and small grants for matching funds (see Acknowledgments for more detail).

Different methods of family selection were more appropriate in this part of the country. In New Mexico, the Japanese American community is small enough to allow for personal contact with a majority of the Japanese American families residing in Albuquerque, Las Cruces, and Gallup. Publicity in local Japanese American newsletters and mailers, as well as word-of-mouth communication, proved productive in finding appropriate families and photographic materials. We also found that some of the publicity initiated in Los Angeles helped locate families in New Mexico because of the well-developed network of communication that links Japanese American families nationally.

Members of the Japanese American community in New Mexico generally agreed that families in Gallup would best represent their interests in the project. Some of these families had resided in New Mexico for the longest continuous period of time, in fact, since the turn of the century. After reviewing the photograph collections of the main Japanese American families in Las Cruces and Gallup, the Uyeda/Miyamura family was selected and invited to participate in the project. Similar to the Nagano sample, their photograph collection was quite extensive and crossed several generations (see Chapter Four), and family members were very interested and enthusiastic about contributing to an understanding of the Japanese American experience in New Mexico.

Methods of Observation and Study

Each case study used similar methods of gathering information. For instance, we did oral histories and many interviews with members of each family. In some cases they were asked to review and discuss their photographs while we listened to and tape recorded their comments. We also borrowed albums and collections of individual photographs for independent inspection and study. In turn, we developed ways to copy, inventory, and catalogue large numbers of pictures for examination and study. We tried to minimize the amount of time that family members were asked to loan their collections to us. We also sought ways to involve family members as active participants in the research process, in the subsequent exhibition of their photographs and comments, and in the future publication of reports about them and their materials. I have included a more complete accounting of these methods and the general research process in Appendix A.

The first framework we used for organizing our case studies was the family history. We quickly realized that our attention to family photographs would be meaningless unless we had a good understanding of the historical details associated with the origin, immigration, and resettlement of each family.

However, we also realized that these individual family histories only made sense in light of a broader framework of historical and cross-cultural influences. A general history of Japanese immigration and settlement in the United States will provide the necessary context. In this way the special circumstances of the Nagano and Uyeda/Miyamura families and relationships to their photograph collections becomes clearer.

Historical Sketch of Japanese Immigration to the United States

During the Tokugawa period (1603–1868) Japan had maintained a self-imposed isolation as a means of maintaining political stability. Japanese immigration to the U.S. began only after the Japanese were forced to sign trade treaties under the threat of American and British aggression (Reischauer 1980: 68, 79). After the restoration of the Meiji Emperor in 1868, the interest in emigration increased, encouraged by the Meiji government's program of Westernization and pushed by local economic conditions in Japanese agricultural communities.

Although many early immigrants to the U.S. mainland were students, labor immigrants generally came from the agricultural prefectures or provinces (*kens*) of western and southern Japan—Hiroshima, Kumamoto, Yamaguchi, Fukuoka, Wakayama, Nagasaki (Wilson and Hosokawa 1980: 48–49). For instance, the Naganos come from the Nagasaki ken and the Uyedas and Miyamuras come from the Kumamoto ken. The high value placed on farming by early immigrants had its roots in the class structure established during the feudal Tokugawa period (1603–1868) (Kikumura 1981: 122). According to historian Edwin O. Reischauer, the natural agrarian bias of feudal society led the political leadership to esteem agriculture (1980: 71).

The change in land ownership from a feudal system to private ownership instituted by the Meiji government created socioeconomic dislocation. Factors such as population growth, poor harvests, industrialization, and a growing number of landless agricultural laborers created a reservoir of labor and a stagnant surplus population—"sufficient to provide the motivation for many to go abroad to secure the money by which a deteriorating family situation might be repressed" (Wilson and Hosokawa 1980: 47). Japanese from these western and southern prefectures were thus provided with ample motivation to emigrate.

Japanese immigration to the U.S. mainland was preceded by immigration to Hawaii beginning in the late 1860s. The majority of Japanese immigrants to the mainland arrived between 1891 and 1924, coinciding with large numbers of Eastern European and Mediterranean immigrants.

Historians speak of two primary periods of Japanese immigration. The first significant wave took place between 1885 and 1907. The *dekasgi* pattern of immigration characterized this period—Japanese laborers intended to go abroad on a temporary basis with full intentions of eventually returning with great wealth. During the Meiji period, the government never envisioned the emigration of permanent labor to the U.S. or elsewhere (Ichioka 1988: 4).

Like the Chinese before them, the Japanese were subjected to racial discrimination and hostility. At the time they entered the U.S., fears of "Asiatics" flooding the country were being kindled by California politicians. Chinese immigration had been unilaterally eliminated by the U.S. Exclusion Act of 1882. In 1906, the attendance of Japanese immigrants in San Francisco public schools escalated into an international conflict, embroiling internal politics on both sides the the Pacific. Negotiations resulted in the "Gentlemen's Agreement" of 1908 by which Japan agreed to restrict severely emigration to the U.S., although wives of Japanese immigrants already in the country were permitted to enter the U.S.

The second wave of immigration began with the Gentlemen's Agreement and ended with the 1924 Immigration Act which was specifically designed to restrict Japanese immigration and to nullify the 1908 agreement. During this time, farming became a principal occupation for Japanese immigrants as well as small businesses, such as hotels, restaurants, barber shops, laundries, curio and art goods establishments, "which became their stake in American society" (Ichioka 1988: 5). The Japanese government also encouraged this shift because, unlike laborers, Issei farmers and businessmen were allowed to call for wives from Japan. Japanese wives then arrived in larger numbers, changing the imbalance between male and female immigrants. Also, during this time period, the "vast majority of pioneer issei women came to the U.S. as wives. These women bore most of their children between 1918 and 1940" (Glenn 1986: 8).

Decades of discriminatory legislation against Japanese in the United States culminated in the Immigration Act of 1924. This act effectively stopped Japanese immigration by designating a zero quota for Japan as part of a dispute that had international repercussions in rising tensions between Japan and the U.S. In the 1922 Takao Ozawa case, the Supreme Court found that only "free white persons" and people of African descent were eligible for citizenship (Ichihashi 1932: 289). By this time, however, resident Japanese immigrants had American-born children, and Japanese American communities had become well established. Although limited by discrimination, the Japanese sojourners became more permanent residents of the United States. In 1920, the U.S.

Census recorded 111,010 Japanese and Japanese American residents, or .01 percent of the total U.S. population (Ichihashi 1932: 104). These figures reflect that the Japanese were never a significant minority in actual numbers of people.

As can be seen from this brief overview, farming was established as the main occupation of prewar Japanese and Japanese Americans. As mentioned, the first Japanese immigrants were bachelors or sojourners who came to improve their family fortunes and return to their homeland. The majority of them settled in California and worked as farmers or farm laborers. While they also filled a need for cheap labor in work for the railroads and in mining, logging, fishing, and meat-packing, they primarily worked in agricultural-related positions.

But beginning in 1913 in California, a string of alien land laws restricted ownership by noncitizens. California "nativist" politicians, rallying public support, also passed a succession of discriminatory laws designed to restrict Japanese land ownership and their economic status. The most significant of this legislation was the California Alien Land Act of 1913 which prevented aliens ineligible for citizenship from owning agricultural property or holding a lease for more than three years. More than eight other states (Washington, Oregon, Idaho, Nevada, Arizonia, New Mexico, Texas and Nebraska) later passed alien land laws (Ichihashi 1932: 280). These land laws took advantage of federal regulations regarding immigration and naturalization by saying that aliens ineligible for citizenship could not own land.

However agriculture-related employment remained central to the immigrant Japanese economy. Simultaneously, growing numbers of Japanese Americans increased their participation in city trades, especially hotels and boardinghouses, restaurants, barbershops, pool rooms, tailor shops, supply stores, shoe shops and so on (Ichihashi 1932: 118–19; Modell 1977:101–11). Interdependent support networks developed within the small Japanese communities. Japanese boardinghouses catered to Japanese workers, sometimes working with their labor contractors. The small businesses sought Japanese suppliers. These family-run businesses became an important institution of Japanese American economic life in urban areas.

The Nagano Family History[3]

The immigration history of the Nagano family is a combination of several unique circumstances and some characteristics that might be classified as typical for Japanese Americans. George's father, Manzo Nagano, was born in 1853 in Kuchino, in the prefecture of Nagasaki, as the fourth of seven children. Not much is known about Manzo's childhood, but we learned that he had gained considerable skill as an apprentice carpenter; he got a job with the captain of a British merchant ship that made trips to Shanghai, China, and to British Columbia. These ships sailed out of Nagasaki, one of the few ports in Japan where foreign ships had been allowed to anchor. The Meiji Restoration (1868–1912) was well under way by the late 1870s; Japan was now open to countries that had been denied access during the Tokugawa era (1603–1868)—a time characterized by cultural and economic isolation and the feudal political control of the Shoguns.

Not being the first-born son, Manzo was left to his own ways. Japanese, in comparison to Anglo-American family traditions, accorded their first-born sons rights and privileges that later sons could not expect. Manzo developed his own sense of adventure, curiosity, and self-sufficiency. In 1877, on one of his trips to Canada he decided to jump ship in Victoria. Manzo was then twenty-two years old, and, as it turned out, the first Japanese to settle in Canada.

According to Tyrus Nagano, one of Manzo's three grandsons, and Steve Nagano, one of his many great-grandsons, Manzo first lived with several groups of Native Americans (no one could recall the specific group) until he learned English. Here he learned local methods of fishing, worked in salmon fishing, and later he introduced gill-net fishing as an alternative technique. Manzo also worked as a lumberjack, and later he worked alongside Chinese immigrants on the construction of the Canadian railroad. This was a common means of employment for many immigrants in both Canada and the United States.

In 1886, when Manzo was thirty-three, he returned to Japan and married Tsuya Ichi, a seventeen-year-old woman from a respectable farming family. They returned to Canada, and four years later, Tsuya gave birth to Manzo's first son, George Tatsuo Nagano, on December 7, 1890. According to Tyrus, Manzo named his son after King George, then titular head of the United Kingdom. Within three years, however, Tsuya died in childbirth, only twenty-three years old. The female child was stillborn. George told his son, Tyrus, that "he almost had a sister." Tsuya Nagano and her daughter were buried together in Oak Cemetery, in Victoria, British Columbia.

Manzo admitted that he could not raise a three-year-old boy by himself. Shortly thereafter, he returned with young George to Japan to find a second wife. While in Yokohama, Manzo started a restaurant that specialized in Canadian and American cuisines. Unlike many of Manzo's other enterprises, this restaurant was not a financial success. However during this time Manzo met and married his second wife, Tayoko Ishii. In 1883, while still in Japan, Tayoko delivered Manzo's second son, Teruo Frank Nagano (see Figure 3).

During the next few years, Manzo expressed a strong desire to return to Canada. However Tayoko was unwilling to leave Japan and her family. It was decided that Manzo should take Tayoko's sister as his wife (as a "step-wife" according to Tyrus) to Canada. So in 1896 Manzo and George returned to Victoria, but Frank remained with his natural mother in Yokohama.

Eleven years later, in 1907, Frank joined Manzo and his wife in Canada as an adopted son. Tyrus Nagano noted that according to Canadian records, Frank was born in Canada. And according to Paul Nagano, another of Manzo's grandchildren, Frank stayed in Canada and moved to Ocean Falls, a community 250 miles north of Vancouver. Frank married Tazuko Uno and had six children—five girls and one boy—all of whom settled in Farnham, Quebec (see Figure 4).

After returning to Canada in 1896, Manzo demonstrated an emerging aptitude for developing his own business. During the Alaskan gold rush in 1897, he established a store that sold equipment and supplies, including buckets, picks, shovels, and food, to ambitious prospectors in the Klondike.

Figure 3. Manzo Nagano family portrait taken by Charlie Wong in Manzo's home on Government Street, Victoria, British Columbia, Canada, in December 1910. Front row, from left to right: Seki Nagano, Manzo Nagano, Tayoko Nagano; Back row, George Tatsuo Nagano, Frank Teruma Nagano. This photograph was published on the front page of *The New Canadian—An Independent Organ for Canadians of Japanese Origin*, on January 8, 1974, accompanying an article entitled "Canada's First Issei," by Toyo Takata, and in *A Dream of Riches—The Japanese Canadians, 1877–1977* (p. 12) as part of the Japanese Canadian Centennial Project, Vancouver, 1978. Courtesy of the George Nagano Family.

Figure 4. Frank and Tazuko Uno Nagano and child taken in Ocean Falls, British Columbia, Canada on March 21, 1937, as it appeared in George Nagano's family album. This part of the family was forced to evacuate to Canada after Pearl Harbor; they stayed in Farnham, Quebec, until 1961. Courtesy of the George Nagano Family.

Building on this financial success, Manzo could afford to continue developing his entrepreneurial talents. He purchased a hotel and started one of the earliest boardinghouses for Japanese laborers. Manzo also opened three stores, one of which was an oriental curio shop located in the same building as his hotel (see Figure 5).

During this time, George attended both Central Elementary School and then North High School, both in Victoria, British Columbia He helped his father in his various enterprises, including fishing, boat-building, and hotel work. George also worked in his father's curio shop when he was sixteen years old.

Manzo took on the role of unofficial consul general, organizing work opportunities and living quarters for Japanese immigrants. He was asked by the Canadian government to travel to Shanghai to enlist Chinese laborers to work on finishing the Canadian railroad.

Manzo prospered in Victoria through the 1920s; his wife proved to be a helpful business partner, and she eventually ran parts of his businesses toward the end of the decade. However, after a serious illness, Manzo returned to Kuchino, Nagasaki in 1923. He died a year later at seventy-one of lung disease, and was buried ten blocks from where he was born.

Manzo's activities in Canada did not go unacknowledged. In 1977 the Canadian government recognized Manzo Nagano as the first Japanese immigrant to Canada. As part of the Canadian Japanese Centennial, a 6,600- foot-high mountain, 300 miles north of Vancouver, was named "Mt. Manzo Nagano."

George's generational status was unusual because of Manzo's immigration history. Manzo's immigration to Canada classifies him as Issei; his son, George, would then be Nisei. But, according to chronological age, George is more appropriately grouped with Issei, and he was first generation in the United States.

As a common practice for Issei males (but less so for Nisei), family friends residing in Japan arranged a marriage for George when he was twenty years old. The result was that in April 1910, a sixteen-year-old woman by the name of Seki Uchiki, who had lived in the prefecture of Tochigi, arrived in Victoria to work for the Naganos. But George did not know Seki had been chosen as his bride until Manzo announced the

Figure 5. The front of Manzo Nagano's Oriental curio shop on Government Street, Victoria, British Columbia, Canada, in June 1911. From left: Mr. Yoshida, "a reporter from Vancouver, British Columbia, Canada *Shimpo*," Manzo Nagano, Tayoko Nagano, and an employee and family friend. (*Shimpo* is a common name for a Japanese newspaper.) Photograph was "taken by George Nagano." Snapshots of family members posing in front of places of work have been common to most Japanese American collections studied for this project. Courtesy of the George Nagano Family.

marriage to him. During the first meeting with his prospective bride, George confessed to Seki that he really "wasn't interested" and that he was more concerned with playing baseball than getting married at the time. George recalled that his stepmother (Tayoko) had arranged the entire matter, that she "said to do this and that and she's the boss. You know. Oh well, it kinda happen so." While recording a life history of George, when he was eighty-eight years old, his daughter, Junko Nagano Morisaku, described this situation as follows:

> The wedding for Tatsuo [George] and Seki was ready, but Tatsuo didn't know [it was] his wedding. He thought that Seki was just another worker from Japan. After two weeks from her arrival, Manzo announced the wedding. Tatsuo was so surprised. He didn't want to get married. But it was Manzo's decision. Nobody could change his decision. They got married in May 18, 1910, at [the] Fujin Home in Victoria. After the ceremony, there was a party at the big hall of the Naganos. While the party was going on, Tatsuo's baseball friends came and asked Tatsuo to go to Vancouver for their baseball games. He left for Vancouver and didn't come home for three days.

This brings us to the first date in the title of George's album, "Nagano's Mother 1910–1952." We see now that these dates do not confine the visual information that is contained in the album. The years of their marriage provide a core period of time to focus the album. However George has provided much additional biographical data that necessarily extends beyond these boundaries.

George and Seki had their first child, Junko Nagano, in 1911, a year after their marriage. According to George, his stepmother wanted her granddaughter to be born in Japan rather than in Canada, and Seki felt that Junko would get a better education in Japan. So, between 1911 and 1914, George lived in Canada and Seki remained in Japan (see Figures 6 and 7). Seki decided that Junko should continue living with Seki's family. Junko did not join her brothers until she moved to the United States fifty-four years later, on June 1, 1965.

The Nagano's first son, Ichiji Tyrus Nagano, was born on May 26, 1915, in Victoria. Five months later, the Nagano family moved to Vancouver. According to Paul and Junko Nagano, George did not get along very well with his stepmother whom he felt favored Frank, his younger stepbrother. During this time, George used his previous store experience and again worked in a curio shop; Seki was also working, taking care of the children of a Reverend Nakagawa. After Seki lived and worked in Vancouver, and George worked in Banff, Alberta, they came to the United States in February 1917 (see Figures 8 and 9).

If Manzo's immigration to Canada had been unique, George's immigration to the United States conformed to a more common pattern. Many Japanese immigrants came to the United States indirectly through Canada after the Gentleman's Agreement in 1908. In response to increased anti-Japanese agitation, and as a voluntary arrangement, the Japanese government discouraged immigration of Japanese laborers to the U.S. Between 1908 and 1913, the number of immigrants was diminished by one-third (Kitano 1969: 28). This agreement also applied to both Canada and Mexico. However, Japanese already in these countries could still enter the U.S. The Nagano family used this provision to move to Ocean Park in Los Angeles County in southern California where they stayed for three years.

Figure 6. A formal portrait of Seki Nagano on the right and her friend and co-worker, "Otoyo-san" taken in December 1913 in Tokyo, Japan, one year before she rejoined her husband in Canada. Seki worked as a telephone operator at the Imperial Hotel in Tokyo. Not only was Seki's work unusual, but her appearance in Western dress was unusual for Japanese women of this period in Japan. Men would appear more often in Western dress with Western accessories such as a bowler hat, umbrellas, and/or Western shoes with their Japanese kimonos, and the women would wear kimonos for formal photographs. Courtesy of the George Nagano Family.

Figure 7. A Christmas card sent by George Nagano from Canada to his wife, Seki Nagano, during her stay in Japan from 1911 to 1914. Here we see one of many examples of how George integrated personal nonphotographic materials into his album. Courtesy of the George Nagano Family.

The Nagano family fit a pattern of indirect immigration or "secondary migrants" to Los Angeles, having lived elsewhere before the U.S. For instance, many Japanese immigrants came through Hawaii, Canada, and Mexico. The first census in 1893 for Los Angeles County listed forty-one Japanese. By 1900 the number was approximately 1,200 followed by 8,461 in 1910, and by 1920, there were already 19,911 Japanese residents in the county, a figure almost four times the number in any other California county (Ichihashi 1932: 108).

During the previous year, 1916, Seki's brother, Henry Uchiki, emigrated from Japan, visited George and Seki in Vancouver, and then went on to California. Thus in 1917 the Naganos came to Ocean Park to assist Henry in a concession stand at an amusement center. George's first job in the U.S. was "cleaning up dishes, cups and drinking glasses" at the Strand Cafe in Venice, California. In the years to come, George and Seki had a long list of jobs and places of work. (See additional detail and discussion in Chapter Three.)

George continued his active interest in athletics, participating in and

Figure 8. A snapshot, dated July 20, 1917, showing George Nagano holding the hand of his first son, Ichiji Tyrus Nagano, who was born in 1915. The photograph was taken between Vancouver, British Columbia, Canada, and Seattle, Washington on board the S. S. *Princess Victoria* during the Nagano's immigration to the United States on their way to San Pedro, California. Courtesy of the George Nagano Family.

Figure 9. George Nagano standing with his co-workers on the "Day Shift at Banff Hotel," July 29, 1916. George worked as a seasonal worker at this hotel in Banff, Alberta, Canada while Seki and Tyrus Nagano remained in Vancouver, British Columbia. Courtesy of the George Nagano Family.

organizing a variety of sports events. He had been an outstanding athlete in high school, playing soccer, basketball, and baseball. In later years, he also learned to play tennis. While in Victoria, British Columbia, George played against visiting baseball teams from Japan, and later, he participated in Japanese American league games in Los Angeles. Paul Nagano remembered that Seki helped by making baseball uniforms for one of George's teams. As a coach for children's neighborhood teams, George became known as "Pops" to many Japanese American youth. This spirit was further demonstrated in the active role he played in the Los Angeles All Nations Boys Club.

Between 1918 and 1942, the Nagano family lived in several homes within and around established Japanese American communities in the Los Angeles area. From their first residence in Ocean Park, they moved in 1918 to the Sierra Madre and La Canada areas. Here George worked in the lemon fields while they lived in labor camps.

Figure 10. George Nagano holding his second son, Kiyoshi Jack Nagano, in Sierra Madre, California, in 1918. The photo was taken in a labor camp in Sierra Madre where George was employed as a laborer, picking lemons. Seki was employed as a cook for the La Canada labor camp (see Kikumura 1981: 28). Courtesy of the George Nagano Family.

In 1918, when Kiyoshi Jack Nagano was born (see Figure 10), they lived in La Canada (central Los Angeles); between 1919 and 1922, they lived in Venice (near Brooklyn Avenue). Their fourth child and third son, Makoto Paul Nagano, was born here in 1920 (see Figure 11). In 1921, the family made a trip back to Victoria, British Columbia, to see George's father Manzo for the last time. They returned to Ocean Park in 1923 to live with Henry Uchiki and his family. The Nagano family also worked with Henry in Compton between 1918 and 1919, during their unsuccessful attempt at farming. The family moved once again in 1924 to 444 East 4th Street (near Omar Street in Little Tokyo). Here they became proprietors of the Mayfair Hotel, a boardinghouse—"for all kinds-for one night" as George described the place. Nine years later, on August 13, 1933, the Naganos moved into their "3rd Street home" (2319 East 3rd Street) in Boyle Heights, East Los Angeles, where they lived until events surrounding World War II forced them to move once again.

After the bombing of Pearl Harbor on December 7, 1941, 120,000 Japanese Americans were forced to alter their life-styles in dramatic and long-lasting ways. George said: "I didn't believe it. . . . I was playing tennis . . . when I looked at a newspaper. . . ." On May 29, 1942, George, Seki, Tyrus, and Paul were interned at the Poston Relocation Center in northern Arizona, where they would stay until November of 1944. Since George was conversant in both Japanese and English, he became manager of Block 35 in Camp I, making him responsible for 300 internees. Seki occupied her time as a sewing instructor, and Tyrus as a custodian. George said: "[Seki] is busy on her sewing, music samisen, and flower arrangement. Rarely she's enjoying her life which she worked so hard nearly all her life; I am glad I can give her rest. It take[s] Poston Arizona to do that."

Jack had married Louise Mizumoto. He was drafted, prior to WW II (see Figure 12), became an officer by 1944, and retired as a lt. colonel. He never had to live in the Poston camps. Paul and other bachelors lived in Camp Three, separated from their families (see Figure 13). Paul married Florence Wake in September 1943, while still living in camp. Paul and Florence left Poston for St. Paul, Minnesota, so that Paul could go to Bethel Seminary and minister to Japanese American sol-

Figure 11. George Nagano in 1918 holding his
third son, Makoto Paul Nagano, on the stairs
of their home in Venice, California, an ocean-
side city that is now part of the metropolis of
Los Angeles. The Naganos found an established Japanese American community here,
since Japanese immigrants had settled early in
this area and San Pedro, establishing small fishing villages (see Modell 1977: 69; Hosokawa
1969: 67–68). Courtesy of the George Nagano
Family.

Figure 12. Louise Mizumoto and Colonel Jack Nagano in a snapshot taken in 1941 at Fort Snelling, Minnesota, an army camp where many Japanese American soldiers received their training. Courtesy of the George Nagano Family.

diers at Camp Savage and Fort Snelling. After the internment period, Paul counselled and assisted Japanese Americans reestablishing their lives on the west coast. George's album indicates that when he, Seki, and Tyrus were released from Poston, they joined Paul and Florence in St. Paul, Minnesota, in November 1943.

George's album also indicates that by December 2, 1945, the Nagano family had returned once again to the Boyle Heights region of Los Angeles. Here George worked as a custodian at the Temple Baptist Church, and Seki did domestic work. Tyrus worked in a department store; Jack was in the Army Reserves while he was employed as a postal worker. As a government-sponsored position, Jack's job was considered a victory in the efforts of Japanese Americans to combat postwar prejudice. And Reverend Paul opened and worked as the pastor of the Japanese (Evergreen) Baptist Church. In 1952, he became the first Executive Secretary for the Japanese Evangelical Missionary Society (JEMS), which he helped found. Seki, George, and Tyrus lived together in their "Folsom Street home" until Seki died suddenly on August 20, 1952—the second date in the title of George's album.

By this date, George and Seki had five grandchildren living in the United States. Jack and Louise had four children; Paul and Florence had three. Junko had remained in Japan and had married Tadashi Morisaku; they had four children (see Appendix B).

In 1970, George retired from his work at the age of eighty. In the life history written by his daughter, Junko, she said: "Tatsuo [George] moved back to his old big house and worked on his albums and scrapbooks. Tatsuo used newspapers, magazines and books for his albums and scrapbooks. He classified all kinds of articles and news. He started keeping his diary from 1916. They were really wonderful works."

In the twenty-seven years from Seki's death to his own, George traveled back and forth between the U.S and Japan, tended his garden, played tennis, watched baseball, and frequented Little Tokyo on a regular basis. In December 1978, George was honored by family and friends in celebration of his eighty-eighth birthday—a special birthday that continues to be recognized in Japanese culture. A year later, three grandsons and two of their friends made the first ascent on Mt. Manzo Nagano. These events were memorable highlights in George's life.

Figure 13. Jack Nagano poses for a snapshot, proudly displaying his status in the U.S. Armed Forces. The caption for this photograph reads: "Last visit home, Camp Robert, Cal[ifornia]." Courtesy of the George Nagano Family.

Steve Nagano has written: "George Tatsuo Nagano died in his Folsom Street home on November 13, 1979, while at his desk, pencil in hand, writing his diary. George is survived by his four children, eleven grandchildren, and eleven great-grandchildren, all of whom live in different parts of the Pacific. Junko and Tyrus are retired, Jack works as a stockbroker, and Paul ministers in Seattle. George's grandchildren live in southern California, Hawaii, and Japan."[4]

The Uyeda/Miyamura Family History

We chose to study the photographic collections of both the Uyeda and the Miyamura families because their histories and current lives are so closely tied to one another. First and foremost, the families are related by blood ties in several generations. The clearest tie occurs in the relationship of the founding patriarchs of the Uyeda/Miyamura family. Heizo Uyeda and Yaichi Miyamura were both *yooshi* (adopted) sons. In Japan, *yooshi* or adoption procedures were not uncommon. If a Japanese family had only daughters, the continuity of the family or *ie* could be assured if: (a) a daughter's (usually the eldest daughter) husband would take her family name, becoming a *muko yooshi*—in this case, Heizo Uyeda (born Iwase) took his wife's family name and became the Uyeda family heir; or (b) a male, often from a related family, would be adopted (personal communication, Elizabeth Chestnut). Yaichi Miyamura was born a Uyeda—as the brother of Tazu Uyeda—but was adopted by the Miyamuras to continue their family name. In addition, these two families considered themselves a separate social group, especially before World War II.

We also learned that the Miyamuras and Uyedas have maintained close ties, even though many of the Nisei and Sansei generation have moved away from Gallup. In some cases, these ties have been maintained through marriage. For instance, Glen Uyeda married Michiko Miyamura Yoshida's sister-in-law, and Gerry Herrera married Patti Teshima. These relationships are clearer when they are presented in diagrams (see Appendix B).

Heizo Iwase was born in 1867, and Tazu Uyeda was born in 1875, both in Ogawa-machi, Kumamoto-ken, Japan. Heizo changed his last

Figure 14. Studio portrait of Heizo (born Iwase) Uyeda taken in Gallup, New Mexico, c. 1905. Solemn facial expressions are very common to both Japanese camera poses and to portraits made at the turn of the century. Courtesy of the Kay Taira Family.

name to Uyeda when he married Tazu in a *yooshi* agreement. They had five children. Frank Kozo Uyeda, also born in Ogawa-machi in 1902, was their fifth child and only son. During the early years of immigration, Hiroshima, Kumamoto, Yamaguchi, and Fukuoka provinces provided the majority of immigrants.

Hiezo, Tazu, and Kozo (later called Frank) Uyeda first arrived in Gallup in 1903 (see Figures 14 and 15). It is not clear why very few Japanese settled in New Mexico. Possible expanations include such factors as the dry climate that discouraged all but subsistence farming, and competition for jobs from the Hispanic American population (Wilson and Hosokawa 1980: 95), as well as remoteness and distance from

Figure 15. Immigration studio portrait of Tazu Uyeda, c. 1900 before arriving in Gallup, New Mexico, in 1903. Courtesy of the Kay Taira Family.

Figures 16 and 17. Two snapshots depicting the living quarters for the coal miners working in Heaton, New Mexico (near Gallup). Chiko's aunt, Tazu Uyeda, operated four boarding-houses for miners; her uncle, Heizo Uyeda, worked as a miner. Courtesy of the Chiko Miyamura Herrera Family.

the west coast. Gallup was then a frontier, Wild West town; Chinese and European immigrants came to Gallup to work as laborers on the railroad, in the coal mines, and in early tourist-related businesses, including restaurants. According to several accounts, the first significant number of Japanese immigrants who entered the U.S. at the turn of the century worked as section hands on the Southern Pacific and Santa Fe railroads (Modell 1977: 26). Wilson and Hosokawa note that in 1906, "perhaps as many as 13,000 Japanese—one in every three in the country—were working for the railroads" (1980: 72). In turn, railroad jobs introduced immigrants to interior geographic areas and other employment opportunities such as farm work. After railroad jobs ended —many Japanese were replaced by Mexicans—"most of these section hands drifted back to the West Coast. But of these thousands a few remained in isolated pockets" (Wilson and Hosokawa 1980: 72).

Gallup was one of the major coal-mining centers in New Mexico. Japanese immigrants began working in the coal mines as contract laborers around 1898.[5] They earned good reputations as reliable workers; Chinese workers before them had not been as welcome, in part because

the men worked and lived without their wives or families. Heizo went to work in the mines while Tazu kept house and cared for Frank. Like other Japanese immigrants who came to Gallup at the turn of the century, the Uyedas [and the Miyamuras] originally worked in the mines and then started small businesses, providing American goods and services. Thus Japanese immigrants who had been rural farmers became small-town tradesmen working in urban settings.

In 1910, Tazu Uyeda started the first of her four very lucrative boardinghouses in mining camps.[6] Miners sank a shaft at Gamerco in 1920 and abandoned the old sites at Weaver, Heaton, and Navajo. The boardinghouses and the miners' homes were moved from Heaton to Gamerco when that camp was opened (see Figures 16 and 17). Tazu housed and looked after as many as 300 miners of all nationalities in these boardinghouses. She closed the Gramerco boardinghouse in 1930 because of the depression.

In terms of Frank Uyeda's age group, he was an Issei (b. 1902). Although he was born in Japan, Frank's experience was characteristic of the Kibei Japanese Americans because he was brought to America

Figure 18. Studio portrait of Frank Kozo Uyeda, c. 1920. By this date, Frank had returned to Gallup after getting a middle school education in Japan.

when he was forty days old, to spend his early childhood in Gallup, and later he was also sent to Heizo and Tazu's home town of Ogawa-machi, Japan, in 1909 for his education. He did not return to Gallup until 1915.

After returning to Gallup, at age thirteen, Frank Uyeda enrolled in the Heaton Elementary School where he quickly relearned English (see Figure 18). He also met his long-time boyhood friend, Richard Fujii. Between 1920 and 1924, while enrolled in the Gallup High School, Frank starred on the football team; he had been on the school baseball team in Japan. While continuing to work in the coal mines during the summer months, he also began to learn auto mechanics and took an active interest in car racing. It was during this time that Frank began teaching himself photography, learning to develop and print his own photographs.

Frank's sister, Kika Uyeda, arrived in Gallup in 1919 and married Joe Matsushita. They had their first child, Kurato, in 1921 (see Figure 19). Joe died in 1926 as the result of a mine-related accident. Kika was re-married in 1927 to George Koyu Taira. The Tairas also opened a series of restaurants in Gallup, called the Eagle Cafe and the Golden Lion Cafe.

In 1924 Frank again left Gallup to study engineering at Purdue University in Lafayette, Indiana. However he relinquished his college education after only one year when he realized his job prospects as an engineer were limited in the United States because he was not an American citizen. His case was not uncommon; many Japanese Americans faced similar prospects:

in the 1930's, when the doors of job opportunity seldom opened for Japanese Americans, Nisei educated as engineers were pumping gas in service stations, business majors helped run the family grocery store, trained teachers went home to the farm or transplanted seedlings in the nursery. It was not at all uncommon for young men who had a Phi Beta Kappa key hidden away in a drawer at home to be working fifteen hours a day in a fruit stand because there was no other employment to be had (Wilson and Hosokawa 1980: 289).

Figure 19. Snapshot of Kurato Matsushita, the son of Frank Uyeda's sister, Kika, seated on a chair covered with a Navajo blanket. This photograph was taken by Frank in Heaton, New Mexico, in 1925. Courtesy of the Grace Tomoko Uyeda Family.

Figure 20. Formal passport photograph of Yaichi [born Uyeda] Miyamura, c. 1906, as found in the "White Album" belonging to Chiko Miyamura (see Chapter 4). Courtesy of the Chiko Herrera Miyamura Family and Shigeko Miyamura.

Frank returned to Gallup where he continued his interests in mechanics, car racing, and photographing Native American life in New Mexico and Arizona.

Shortly after his return to Gallup in 1925, he married a Japanese Hawaiian woman, Koto, who had been educated at the University of Hawaii. She died of tuberculosis shortly after the birth of their son, Glen, in 1930. Frank was remarried the following year to Grace Tomoko Terasaki, a Nisei from Hawaii, also known to family members as Tomoko-san. And in 1932, they had a daughter, June Uyeda. During the following years, Frank worked in various automotive garages in and around Gallup. Grace still resides in Gallup as does their daughter, June Uyeda Kauzlarich, and her family.

In 1930, Frank's parents, Tazu and Heizo, returned to Ogawa-machi, their home town in Japan; Heizo died in 1933, Tazu in 1942. Frank remained in Gallup and died of a heart attack in 1968.

Yaichi Uyeda was Tazu's younger brother. He was born in 1888 in the same town as Tazu and Heizo, Ogawa-machi, Japan. He became a Miyamura as part of another *yooshi* arrangement, this time adopted as an anticipated family heir. In 1906, Yaichi emigrated to the United States, stopping first in Seattle (see Figure 20); after three years of searching for Tazu and Heizo along the railroad lines and depots in Wyoming, Montana, and Utah, he arrived in Gallup, New Mexico.

Like Frank, Yaichi also returned to Japan in 1912; but unlike Frank, he was drafted into military service, being stationed in Korea. Later, in 1918, he married Tori Miyamura (born in 1896) in Ogawa-machi (see Figure 21) and began an unpleasant period of farming with his wife's family. They started their family in Japan in 1920 with the birth of Chiyoko (Chiko), the first of their seven childen (see Figure 22). The following year they all returned to New Mexico, first to Raton, then to Gamerco, Heaton, and Gallup.

After Yaichi worked in the mines for another short period of time, in 1923 he and Tori started a restaurant in a railroad car, appropriately called the "Box Car Lunch." This year coincided with the beginning of the Gallup Ceremonial—an important thrust in developing the local

Figure 21. Formal studio portrait taken as part of the 1918 wedding of Yaichi [Uyeda] Miyamura and Tori Miyamura in Japan. Courtesy of the Chiko Herrera Miyamura Family.

Figure 22. Tori Miyamura holding her daughter Chiyoko (Chiko) in a studio-made commemorative or *Kinen Shashin* photograph, marking their departure for America in 1920. Courtesy of the Chiko Miyamura Herrera Family.

Figure 23. Frank demonstrated his interest in Native American life by taking photographs of local events like the annual Gallup Ceremonial, c. 1923. He also included postcards from Indian reservations in his album. Courtesy of the Chiko Miyamura Herrera Family.

tourist ecomony (see Figure 23). Yaichi then opened the "OK Cafe" in 1929, a large restaurant, open twenty-four hours a day, catering to the needs of their clientele—Native Americans, townspeople, and a slowly growing tourist population.

Yaichi sold the OK Cafe and bought the "Lucky Lunch" after the death of his wife, Tori, in 1936. The Lucky Lunch was smaller, and it was easier for him to raise their seven children, Chiyoko, Momoko, Michiko, Hershey, Suzuko, Kei, and Shigeko, ages four to sixteen, while continuing to run his restaurants. Chiko, the eldest daughter, also had responsibility for caring for her brothers and sisters and working in the restaurant. Yaichi owned and operated the Lucky Lunch between

Figure 24. Yaichi Miyamura poses for a snapshot with his grandson, Jerry Herrera, Jr. ("Babe") as they stand next to the daily menu in the Lucky Lunch Restaurant, one of the Miyamura family's three restaurants in Gallup, New Mexico. Courtesy of the Chiko Herrera Miyamura Family.

1940 and 1963 (see Figures 24 and 25). In 1963 he turned the operations and ownership of this restaurant over to Chiko. He then left for California to stay with his other daughters, Momoko and Michiko. At seventy-eight years of age, Yaichi died in California, and his body was returned to Gallup to be buried next to Tori.

Unlike the Naganos, neither the Uyeda nor the Miyamura families was forced into internment camps after Pearl Harbor. New Mexico was not in the Western Military Defense Zone. The U.S. government left decisions up to individual towns and communities. Gallup's City Council voted against relocation of Gallup's Japanese American residents.

In the Issei and Nisei generations, the two families remained close, particularly because a strong friendship developed between Frank Uyeda and Yaichi Miyamura (see Figure 26). Presently, members of both families see or communicate with one another on a regular basis. Yaichi's sons and daughters are particularly close, so that when they speak of the Miyamura family, it includes all of Yaichi's Nisei children, their children, and grandchildren. Unlike many traditional Japanese families, Yaichi's children did not become strangers. A shift from the vertically oriented patrilineal pattern to one that featured bilateral and horizontal relationships was not uncommon for Japanese American families. Yanagisako remarks that Issei and Nisei have not followed the Japanese adage "The sibling is the beginning of the stranger." Horizontal links of siblinghood seem to have replaced vertical links of filiation (1985: 196). If anything, Issei insisted that people stay in touch and informed:

> *Issei women by and large kept in close written communication with their siblings in Japan, particularly their sisters. Indeed, women tended more than men to follow consciously the lives of their siblings and their children through the exchange of letters and, when they could afford them, small gifts (1985: 197).*

In fact, the sisters' husbands were incorporated into the extended family. The photographs we found in the Gallup collections reflect this family organization.

Figure 25. One of several self-portrait snapshots of Yaichi Miyamura seated at a table in the Lucky Lunch Restaurant in Gallup, New Mexico. Courtesy of the Chiko Herrera Miyamura Family.

The Uyeda/Miyamura family is an unusual Japanese American family because they did not settle in a large ethnic community on the West Coast. As of 1930, California listed 87,456 Japanese American residents, 35,390 of which were in Los Angeles County, while New Mexico recorded only 249 (Ichihashi 1932: 96, 99). This family decided to remain somewhat isolated in an inland context. The Uyeda/Miyamura family comes from a setting—a small western rural town—where family activities center around the home, and the family is well known. For instance, Chiko married a Gallup Spanish American of Basque descent, John Herrera; and Hershey returned to Gallup after military service in World War II to marry Terry.[7]

The scale of most organizations and institutions in Gallup is small when compared to the Los Angeles area. For less urbanized families, cross-cultural exchange and adaptation were virtually inevitable. Such changes were reinforced as families like the Uyeda/Miyamuras grew, and new generations settled not only in Gallup but also in other parts of the United States. In Gallup, Japanese American families encountered the cross-ethnic influences of three main cultures—Anglo American, Spanish, and Native American. Abundant employment opportunities

Figure 26. From left to right, Frank Uyeda, his younger sister, Kika Uyeda Taira, and their uncle, Yaichi [born Uyeda] Miyamura holding his camera, as they appeared in 1964. This photograph is part of Chiko Miyamura's "White Album" (see Chapter Four). Courtesy of the Chiko Herrera Miyamura Family.

helped Gallup develop a reputation for an unusually warm welcome of immigrants (see Figure 27). So that by the turn of the century, Japanese Americans found themselves in the presence of twenty-four different ethnic groups that settled in this relatively small geographic area. Some of Chiko Miyamura Herrara's comments addressed this point:

> *Gallup is unique as a city or town because of the different races (ethnic groups) in Gallup. And most of them were immigrants to begin with from years back. . . . No one race or nationality was financially [well-off] . . . everybody worked hard. Everybody knew each other, so that made Gallup a good town to live in.*

About Japanese Americans, she commented:

> *The Japanese Americans here . . . they weren't so together. They didn't stay as a group. Like we went to Japanese school . . . with the rest of the kids, but then, once we got out of Japanese school, we go run off and play with someone else. Of course, I had to go back to work. But, I know the kids all played with different nationalities. Kei, Hershey, all of them had Italian friends, Anglo friends; they used to fight with the Indians.*

As an example of living in a multiethnic community, Michiko Yoshida, one of Chiko's younger sisters, discussed the effects of learning more about Japanese culture after getting married:

> *you're born with that certain, certain trait. And of course, being that we never associated with Japanese in Gallup as much, other than just our relatives, so it was really quite a new experience for my sister and all of us after we got in where there is a big majority of Japanese and mingling with different ones, so therefore a lot of the Japanese history and culture we learned after we married our husbands, and associating with more Japanese.*

The Japanese American population in Gallup continues to recognize itself as a community in spite of an emerging pattern of intermarriage to several groups, mostly Hispanic and Native American.

Figure 27. Dancing School Recital from Gallup, New Mexico, c. 1932. Two of Frank Uyeda's nieces, Mary Taira and Kay Taira (daughters of Kika Uyeda Taira), appear first and second from the right. This portrait offers a nice example of how various ethnic groups were generally well integrated in Gallup. Courtesy of Kay Taira.

New Mexico and California

As we anticipated, it became quite clear that family history, settlement location, and variation in Japanese American culture are intimately related. By selecting families from different regions of the United States, we gained some indication of how groups sharing the same ethnic identity may differ from one another. For instance, when Michiko was talking about her father, Yaichi Miyamura, in relation to regional differences and associated processes of acculturation, she said:

> *And most of the Isseis [did not say that much]—this is why when we got married it was kind of hard to [know traditions] really, being that we didn't know too much about the Japanese really—as much as the people on the West Coast. It [getting married] was quite educational for us, also. You know, because we were not aware of a lot of other things that were the culture of the Japanese. I mean, I guess my father couldn't teach us everything or tell us everything, but the main things he sure did: "Work hard get good grades." Which we did.*

And later:

> *Well, living in New Mexico and living in California, there's two very different—because being among the Japanese more and in a larger group [in L.A.] and then in Gallup, where it's just among the relatives and everything, I think it's been very educational and not everybody has the opportunity to live where the actual Indian reservations are and learn about their culture. And I feel that I've received a very good education in living—being brought up in New Mexico, and then learning about my own Japanese heritage and everything, which was educational for me after marrying a Japanese from California.*

When Chiko compared Gallup to West Coast communities, she observed that "They didn't mingle with other races. . . . They just didn't. . . . [We did] maybe because we're a small town. It's just too much to be around Japanese kids only, that you got to get away from them sometimes, get around with other kids. . . ."[8] We also heard Grace Uyeda comment on how this pattern of multiethnic interaction is maintained in contemporary times:

> *Oh, I have all different kinds [of friends]. I have Mexican friends, Japanese, Chinese living by me, white people, Indian friends. This Indian boy that used to work for us in the garage, he lives up in Zuni, you know, about fifty miles from Gallup. Once in a while he comes to see Gallup and he comes to see me.*

Chiko's and Grace's comments were very interesting, since we found so many photographs of their Anglo, Hispanic, Italian, Japanese, and Native American friends in their albums.[9]

Using the Nagano and Uyeda/Miyamura family histories as a kind of baseline, we attempted to understand better how their pictorial records are both family and culture specific. What specific moments in the history of each family have received pictorial attention? In some ways we were asking how people use a photograph album to illustrate a life, and how members of these two Japanese American families used their photographs to retain and communicate historical, personal, social, and cultural information. In short, how did they record, construct, and communicate their personal histories? From the two case studies discussed in the following chapters, we found that Japanese Americans answered these questions in different but related ways.

Chapter Three

George Nagano's Family Album

While studying the Nagano family history, we were struck by the observation that so much historical detail was available in the photograph collection of George Nagano. We were indeed fortunate to have information from both the still photographs and the captions that accompany so many of them. Our review indicated that George intentionally structured his pictures as a statement of personal history, as a pictorially realized model of life history. Clearly he was fond of keeping track of detail and organizing bits and pieces of information into meaningful statements. These observations prompted us to learn more about George as a photographer and keeper of the family history.

George Nagano as Family Photographer and Archivist

All of George's sons remember their father as an avid photographer, as a person who just enjoyed taking pictures for personal reasons and pleasure. We learned that throughout George's adult life, he maintained a written personal history through annual diaries. By Steve Nagano's estimates, his grandfather put together as many as thirty or forty scrapbooks on such topics as "Relocation," the Rose Bowl Parades, the look of American women, and the Nisei baseball leagues. George surprised his family when they discovered that in 1977, two years before his death, he began organizing his own will in scrapbook form. We also know he made several albums from his enormous collection of photographs. When we asked Paul Nagano why his father took so many photographs, he replied: "My Dad . . . he enjoyed writing. He used to write a lot of letters, so I can think, the idea of keeping a journal was a type of posture in life that caused him to take pictures, record this, record that. . . ." Later we asked Paul if he remembered his father actually taking pictures and the kind of cameras he used:

> *Oh, I wish we'd kept that. He had a box camera, Eastman box camera, like that. . . . I wonder whatever happened to that. But anyway, he used to take that with him everywhere. And I have a lot of images of him rolling that film in there. . . . He'd put a back lid on it, so it remained dark. And I think it took only ten or twelve pictures. . . . And he would take that with him—just a little cheap Eastman camera, in this little square box. . . . On the side of this box, there's a little trigger, "click," and then he'd wind it and then there's a little opening there, and you can tell it comes to the next number, then it's ready for the next shot. . . . It was a cheapie, but it took good pictures.*

When our project director, Lynne Horiuchi, asked: "How did you feel about his taking pictures all the time of you boys?" Paul replied:

> *It became a life-style. Just part of his being, he had that camera with him all the time . . . so that, he was at a restaurant, he'd have a waitress or waiter take our picture—he'd give them the camera [and say] "All you have to do is click this." I still remember that. Every place he'd go. It was a little embarrassing, probably. . . .*

George's Album: "Nagano's Mother 1910–1952"

Given a brief life history and an introduction to George as the family photographer, we can better examine the structure and content of one of George's albums, one that became the center of our attention. Entitled "Nagano's Mother 1910–1952," this album contains a total of 635 items placed on 137 pages (see Figures 28 and 29). The dates in the album's title include the years that George was married to Seki Nagano. By many standards "Nagano's Mother 1910–1952" is a remarkable piece of work, integrating a rich collection of pictorial and written materials. But we should be able to say more by identifying the

Figure 28. Cover of 137-page album made by George Nagano. From the very start, we get a sense of how George added personal touches to materials he had available, creating an original and meaningful document. We do not believe the "OZ" on the album's front cover and binding had any significance to George. Apparently he recycled a commercial binder that was used as a catalog of sample greeting cards. Courtesy of the George Nagano Family.

cultural significance of the album through an understanding of how this album functions both as a multichanneled vehicle of communication and as a structured pattern of pictorial information. In this case, how is it structured? What kinds of communication are involved, and how does it work?

Several structural and organizational features of this album are very revealing. To the best of our knowledge, George formally organized this album in 1960, eight years after Seki's death. We are certain he had been planning its contents years before this date. George chronicles his life with Seki with at least one page for each year they were married. His chronological order is created by pasting cut-out numbers of the year on the left-hand corner of the page (see Figure 30). We also know that George reworked the album in several ways between 1960 and 1978. For instance, he amended and supplemented both the visual and verbal components several times. Inserting pages of photographs from his other albums had the effect of extending the time frame from 1952

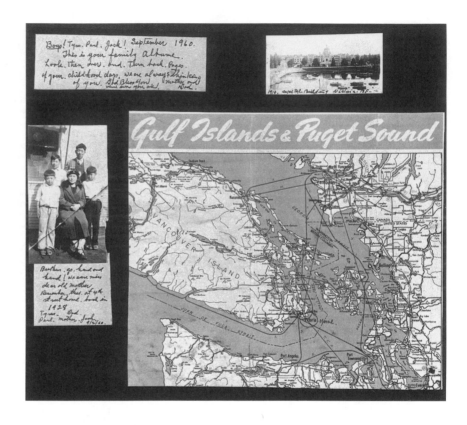

Figure 29. Inside front cover of "Nagano's Mother 1910–1952." George provides an introduction to the contents of his album by writing instructions for its use by the Nagano children and by including a map of Vancouver and Puget Sound indicating the geographical-historical context of the family origins in North America. Courtesy of the George Nagano Family.

to 1978. He also placed more recent photographs on the original album pages, inserted newspaper clippings, and added new captions or embellished old ones. The effect is one of continuously contributing more detail to his accounts.

We also found that George's album contained many kinds of photographic imagery. Professional studio portraits, professionally made wedding photographs, team pictures, and public relations photographs have been combined with his amateur snapshots. There are also pictures clipped from magazines, newspapers, and brochures combined with postcards.

The verbal qualities of album communication are equally important.

Figure 30. An example of how George created year-by-year chronology in "Nagano's Mother 1910–1952." This page includes captioned snapshots and comments detailing specific events and activities that occurred during 1952, the year George's wife, Seki Nagano, died in Los Angeles, California. Courtesy of the George Nagano Family.

Almost all images in Geoge's album are accompanied by a variety of written captions and citations in English; some of these appear in the borders, or they are written on small pieces of white paper. In addition, there are short newspaper articles written in both Japanese and English. We also found maps, Christmas cards, and advertisements for a photography store and a mortuary, among other services and businesses. In other words, rather than just a random collection of snapshots, we are working with a highly selective and well-integrated collection of visual and verbal forms.

We previously stated that "Nagano's Mother 1910–1952" is dedicated to George's wife, Seki, to whom he was married from 1910 until

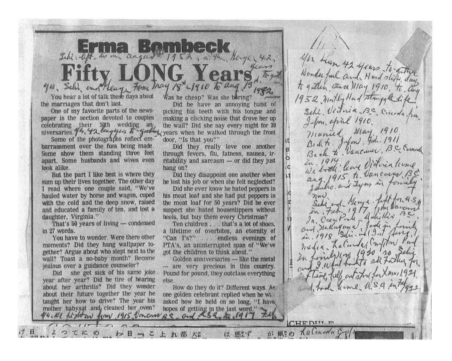

Figure 31. George also supplemented his album with clippings published in magazines, brochures, and newspapers—articles that directly revealed his own thinking and feelings about his life with Seki, his wife for forty-two years. Courtesy of the George Nagano Family.

her death in 1952. Assembling this album in 1960, it appears that George vicariously celebrated his fiftieth wedding anniversary through this activity. George makes a reflective comment on the significance of this anniversary by including an Erma Bombeck newspaper column about the achievement of staying married for fifty years (see Figure 31). He accompanied this clipping with the following remarks: "Yes, 42 long years together. . . . Yes, Seki and George from May 18th to Aug(ust) 13th, 1952. . . . Been 42 years together. . . . Wonderful and hard ship days together. . . . Mostly hard struggle life." When George writes comments on articles such as this Erma Bombeck column, he seems to be conducting simultaneous dialogues with the column's author and Seki Nagano as well as his children and future viewers of his album.

"Nagano's Mother 1910–1952" presents us with a dense text—one that interweaves many sources, producing an account full of intentional juxtapositions of information—an extremely rich narrative form. In these ways, we find indisputable evidence that George fully intended to create a statement, to construct a particularized view and interpretation of life to be learned and appreciated by his children and future Nagano generations.

George's Album as a Model of Interpersonal Communication

Next we should explore evidence for the model of interpersonal communication that George had in mind when he made the album. This type of information is usually left to implicit layers of understanding. One cultural assumption we make about family albums is that they are for viewing, interpretation, education, and enjoyment of family members, close relatives, and, possibly, intimate friends. In this regard, dedications, author's acknowledgments, prefaces, forewords, and other types of introductory information, generally found in published books, are not thought to be necessary in photograph albums.

But George seems to break this pattern. He is consistently explicit in his family album, offering sets of communication instructions. For example, on the inner cover of the album (see upper left corner of Figure 29), he writes: "Boys! Tyrus, Paul, Jack—This is your family albums. Look them over and Turn back Pages of your childhood days. We are always thinking of you. God Bless you where ever you are. Mother and Dad." As we search further we find that this initial directive is only one of several instructional devices used throughout the album. George uses his album to make three different and sometimes overlapping kinds of statements to communicate to (1) to his children, (2) to his wife, Seki, after her death, and (3) to himself, as a kind of note-taking. A few examples will clarify these lines of communication.

In communicating to his children, George uses the album as a message form to tell his three boys about Seki or "Mother." George's comments on Seki's life are often explicitly directed toward his sons. This information (originally) provides Tyrus, Paul, and Jack (and later

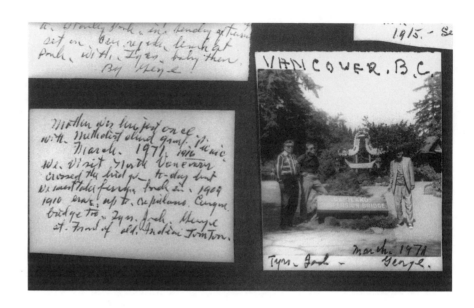

Figure 32. From left, Tyrus Nagano, Jack Nagano, and George Nagano appear in a snapshot taken "in front of [an] old Indian Tom Tom" in Vancouver, British Columbia, Canada, in March 1971. George added this photograph and its annotation to his original album to elaborate on Seki Nagano's life history. Courtesy of the George Nagano Family.

Junko) with contextual, personal knowledge about their mother. For example, next to a photograph of Tyrus, Jack, and George taken at Vancouver, British Columbia, George writes: "Mother was here just once with Methodist Church group picnic . . . in 1916. . . ." (see Figure 32). On a page dedicated to the year 1952, the year that Seki passed away (see upper left corner of Figure 30), George writes: "Mothers final year. She passed on August of this year. We all miss her. Do not forget to visit her grave, boys. Wonderful Mother to us all—Dad." Other examples of captioned information chronicle Seki's activities. The following three comments come from a much longer list of separate captions (see Figures 33, 34, and 35): "Issei and Nisei Church where Seki use[d] to go every Sunday. Mother used to walk home often [on[4th Street from Hollenbeck Ball ground. Seki always came here, [to] buy Japanese tofu." These examples represent explicit forms of messages and information. The album is also full of implicit forms of information directed toward the children but in less obvious manners—for purposes of educaton and socialization.

Figure 33. A view of the Evergreen Playground as seen in a snapshot taken by George Nagano in April 1968. Located in the Boyle Heights section of East Los Angeles, George writes that this setting is near an Issei and Nisei church "where Seki use[d] to go every Sunday." Reverend Paul Nagano was pastor of the Evergreen Baptist Church. George also uses this caption to point out a place ("see tennis court") where, according to other accounts, he spent many good times as both a tennis player and coach. Courtesy of the George Nagano Family.

We also find George using his album to make statements to Seki after her death. Many of the photographs he used in this manner were taken after Seki's death. George uses pictures and captions as channels of communication. In this way he speaks to Seki and shows her familiar places, events, and objects. This was George's way of updating her knowledge of important family matters—keeping Seki a member of the family. Most of the following examples come from the pages of pictures that George added to the first version of his album. For instance, under a church photograph (see Figure 36), we read: "Mother remember Union Church. You went [to] Many Service[s] here. Sometimes late at night." Similar references to being at Union Church are made in two other photographs (see Figure 37). Under a picture of Tyrus holding his niece, Nowa (Junko's granddaughter) on his lap (see Figure 38), we read: "Remember Mother Tyrus was Noria['s] age when we left Vancouver, B.C. Canada for USA." In a related example (see Figure 39), we find the following caption: "Remember Mitsuba Cafe Mother. We visit here sometimes [for] Sunday supper Tyrus [is a] big boy now. George" Another one (see Figure 40) refers to Paul's family: "Mother this is Paul's family. [Their] Visit at Folsom Home. . . . Mother, all big boys, now." And still later (see Figure 41): "Mother, this is family get together today—we all miss you at your Home. Mother . . . all are very Happy."

In these and several other examples, George has used his album to maintain communication with family members who have either moved or passed away. The making and sharing of personal photographs extends the possibilities of "being together" to at least a personal sense of "staying in touch." We found many examples of this same theme in the materials from the other family in our project. The Uyeda/Miyamuras used their photographs to maintain a family unity and share information, but in a greater variety of ways.

George Nagano used his own photographs and other images to report specific changes that occurred since George and Seki saw some place, person, or event together. Again, most of these annotations appear on loose album pages, most of which were added to the first version of the album during the late 1960s and early 1970s. For example,

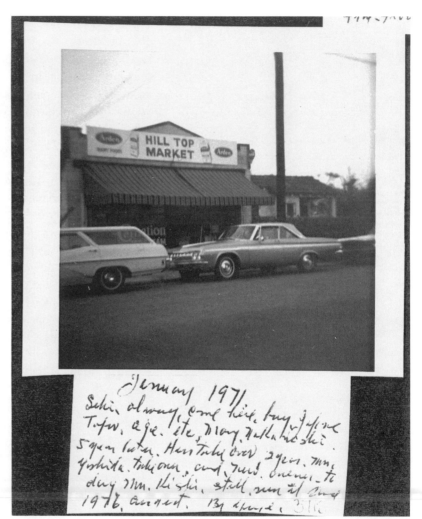

Figure 34. George included a snapshot of an area known as "Hollenbeck Playground," (a part of Hollenbeck Park in Boyle Heights), a place also familiar to Seki. George added a descriptive detail in his caption, writing their "3rd st home [was] near here," offering viewers a greater sense of familiarity and geographical context. Courtesy of the George Nagano Family.

Figure 35. George Nagano took this snapshot in January 1971, and placed it in his album to illustrate another place familiar to Seki during their marriage. The caption notes that Seki frequently did her household food shopping here. In George's penchant for detail, he even listed the sequence of people who owned the Hill Top Market. Courtesy of the George Nagano Family.

Figure 36. Color snapshot of front of Union Church, located in Little Tokyo, Los Angeles, taken by George Nagano during Nisei Week, on August 24, 1968. We are given another example of how George retraced Seki's footsteps and photographed familiar and significant locations. Courtesy of the George Nagano Family.

Figure 37. Still another color snapshot that reinforces George and Seki's church affiliation and a repeated reference to the church fence. George's caption reads: "March, 1973. Seki was here many times. Remember the old Union Church Fence. There for many years." The Union Church became a significant location for Japanese Americans: "Considered quite a showplace in central Little Tokyo, the Union Church became the core of community activities, including many of the 'social church' variety" (Modell 1977: 77). Courtesy of the George Nagano Family.

Figure 38. Junko Nagano Morisaku took this color snapshot of Tyrus Nagano holding her granddaughter, Nowa, in George and Seki's Folsom Street home in Boyle Heights, Los Angeles, in March 1972. Courtesy of the George Nagano Family.

Figure 39. Tyrus Nagano and George Nagano seated for a color snapshot taken by "Susie Waitress" in June 1974. Unlike most photographs in Anglo American albums, pictures made in restaurants were found in both Japanese American collections studied for this project. After Seki's death, George used captions for photographs like this to update Seki on his choice of restaurants, sometimes reminding her of their good times together. Courtesy of the George Nagano Family.

Figure 40. A three-generation color snapshot taken by Tyrus Nagano in his father's Folsom Street home in June 1974. George purposefully placed this picture in his album to report the status of Paul's family to Seki. We see grandfather George Nagano in the center with his grandchildren Jimmy and Janet on the left and Steve on the far right; George's son, Paul, stands to the right of his father. Courtesy of the George Nagano Family.

Figure 41. Another three-generation color snapshot taken by Tyrus in April 1976. The occasion is "a family get-together"—showing George and his daughter, Junko, and five of his grandchildren. Another "miss you Mother (Seki)" message appears in George's caption. Courtesy of the George Nagano Family.

Figure 42. George Nagano and "Kuno-san," a good friend of the Nagano family. Color photograph was taken in February 1973, at Zenshuji Temple, and placed and captioned in George's album in December 1977. Courtesy of the George Nagano Family.

Figure 43. George even photographed the spot where Seki got off the street car on the way to her 3rd Street home. Again George writes a caption to recount the details and significance he saw in a particular view: "Mother got off st[reet] car here from down town—not much change. No stand like used to [be]." Without this captioned information, we, and possibly family members, would not know why the photograph was included in this album. Courtesy of the George Nagano Family.

under a photograph of a garden area, we read: "March 1971. We Visit Victoria B C Canada, Our second visit since 1921. Big Change. Not much Japanese here now. . . . Our old brick building gone now not much Japanese here. . . . I like to take Junko here. . . . This might be my last visit to my Home town."

Under a photograph of George and his good friend and neighbor (see Figure 42), Mrs. Kuno, we read: "But today Mrs. Kuno sold her home and moved away from Folsom. Today is December 1977 less Japanese around here now, about 6 family[ies]. Use[d] to be 10 or more." In another caption, we read: "Pershing Square. remember at that center fountain back in 1947 now its gone. Big change here in Sept 1962" And under a picture of a car and street corner (see Figure 43), we read: "Remember 3rd Street Home. Mother get[s] off St [street] Car here from downtown, not much Change. No store like use[d] to, but same station now."

By reporting events in this manner, we might surmise that George is addressing himself as if keeping a notebook or diary of his own thoughts and reflections. It could be argued, in fact, that much of George's caption-writing is similar to keeping daily diaristic entries. We do know that he kept annual diaries for over forty years. Attention to daily ritual, prayers, and personal observation as part of daily life is an important value that the Issei brought with them from Japan.

But it is equally significant to realize that George's behavior follows the Japanese custom of treating recently departed relatives to whom one is very close as a continuing part of everyday life. For instance, anthropologist Robert Smith reported in his book, *Ancestor Worship in Contemporary Japan,* that it is common for the living to speak directly to the deceased, represented by a tablet and a photograph placed in a household altar. People regularly report on a variety of family matters: the status of the family business, making changes in the layout of the house, recent births and marriages, illnesses, and passing the entrance examination for college (Smith 1974: 143). In another study from Japan, anthropologist David Plath includes the following comment in his discussion of "memorialism": "The souls of all household

members should be treated as though alive. . . . The wants of the
departed soul can be catered to directly. . . . One can visualize the departed in explicit form. One also can use photographs to heighten the
effect" (1964: 308–9). In these examples George is maintaining an on-
going relationship with Seki, using the album photographs as a channel
of communication and as a medium of interpersonal expression.[1]

This communicative technique is important for its apparent relationship with and, indeed, adherence to Japanese patterns of behavior as
discussed by Smith and Plath. George appears to be satisfying a cultural
value placed on informing people from the "past." But George is also
communicating information to people in the "future." This strategy
resembles what Takie Lebra refers to as "refracted communication."
Lebra gives the following example: "If Ego feels intimacy toward a deceased kin, say, his mother, Ego may talk aloud to her in front of the
household shrine or gravestone, so that Alter, with whom Ego really
wants to communicate, will hear" (1976: 122). It would appear that
George is using his family album in this pattern of communication.
By directing comments about the present to some one in the past, he
is offering information to people in the future. Here we find one way
George incorporated themes of continuity and change into his album
narrative and, in doing so, appears to get the best of two (or possibly
more) worlds. By placing these captions within his album, his statements of change are contributing to a continuity in information for
contemporary and future family members.

Both the pattern and content of George's communication present us
with the first references to two themes that will unify elements of the
remaining chapters, namely the Japanese concept of *ie* and the notions
of belonging and membership (see Chapter Five). Both illustrate ties
between communication and cultural transmission. By reporting information to his children and to his departed wife, George was expressing
a strong need to keep pieces of the family unit together through time
and maintaining an awareness of identity and interpersonal relationships. Many additional examples given on the following pages will echo
these themes.

Intrapersonal Features of Communication in George's Album

Another form of communication includes a person's comments on what that person said or otherwise expressed—sometimes referred to as communication about communication or "meta-communication." This usually occurs when a speaker, author, performer, or photographer calls explicit attention to the existence or production of the presentation. We found several kinds of this type of communication in George's album. For instance, George has included written annotations that either identify the photographer or clarify details of the picture-taking activity. Examples include: "by George," "by Tyrus," "by Susie Waitress," "Seki took pictures here," and "one of four last pictures together" (see Figures 44 and 45). In a more elaborate expression (see Figure 46): "May, 1942—Paul, George, Tyrus, Mother leave for Poston Center while Kiyoshi [Jack] in Army. He took this picture. no pictures taken [in] camp. So this was last one at a time. Paul left for Camp after this was taken on May 24, 1942." Other examples are directed toward an evaluation of the photograph or its significance: "Few of best Family Picture[s] . . ." (see Figure 47) or "One of good Pictures of Mother [at] Paul's home" (see Figure 48). In other cases, George records information about the making of his album: "In year 1979 February I put in album" (see Figure 49).

And finally, two other comments include reference to what George was thinking while he viewed the album, producing the effect of George talking to himself: "Today I check on Mother's album and find memories. . . . [A]lso look over Mother's Photo Book Album. Memories come back of those days in St. Paul Minn[esota]. . . . Yes we all miss our dear mother."

All of these examples develop a pattern of discourse that is similar to what Lebra describes as "self-communication" and would seem to satisfy traditional needs to keep diaries of detailed observations:

> *Ego may write down his thoughts and wishes as if he were doing so to his own satisfaction. This may take the form of a diary—a possible*

Figure 44. George's caption reads "Saturday Aug. 24, 1968 Big Parade. Nisei Week on Sunday. This is Little Tokyo decorated. George took this from front of Merit bank." Courtesy of the George Nagano Family.

explanation for the Japanese habit of keeping a diary. The writer feels free to express his sentiments, for he is communicating with himself alone. The style of writing will be that of the monologue. . . . Such self-communication can become socially significant if it is ever disclosed. In some instances, disclosure is expected by the writer (1976: 123–24).

Readers should note, first, that diary-writing has been a Japanese literary form for years, including the "zuihitsu" style (Dalby 1984: 74). Second, we would have to agree that photograph albums—communicative forms—are meant to be discovered. The information in this album is intended to go in two directions—to George, as if he was talking to himself, and toward present and future family members, but in less direct ways. Again, George's intentions appear to be keeping people informed and together. We find more evidence for how George's album promotes the communication of unity and stresses the theme of belonging—themes that will be discussed in greater detail in Chapter Five.

Album and Photograph Content as Communication

We have discussed how the explicit intent to communicate information has structured George's creation of his family album. We have noticed the persistence of an active process and network of people "speaking" and being "spoken to." We now turn our attention to issues of content—to what is being communicated through this family album as a message form. As discussed in Chapter One, this collection of information is best understood as an interpretation of life and culture. Here we want to know how the album contains both reports and interpretations of what George experienced or saw, where and how he decided to point his camera, and also what he had to say about his choices in both pictorial and written forms. Four themes appear with great regularity throughout his album—matters related to work/labor, religious/church activities, funerals/death, and last times/farewells. George celebrated the significance of these topics through his photographs and captions; he interpreted these themes in ways that are uncommon in Anglo American albums.

Figure 45. From left, top row, Jack Nagano and George Nagano; bottom row, Paul Nagano and Tyrus Nagano. Caption reads: "one of four last pictures together in 1941." George draws attention to "last times" throughout his album (see additional comment later in this chapter). Courtesy of the George Nagano Family.

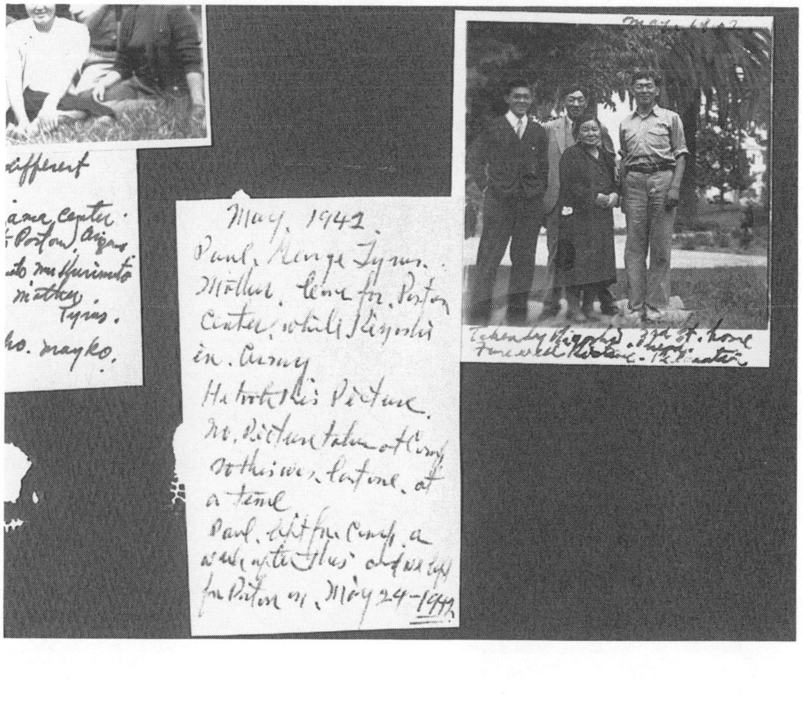

Figure 46. Paul Nagano, George Nagano, and Tyrus Nagano standing behind "mother" Seki Nagano in a snapshot taken by Jack Nagano in May 1942 just before they left Los Angeles to be interned in the Poston Camp in Arizona. Again, George calls attention to a "last time." Courtesy of the George Nagano Family.

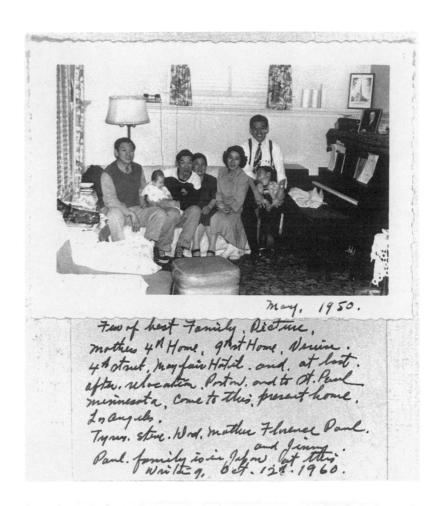

Figure 47. Nagano family gathering—from left: Tyrus, Steve, George, Seki, Florence, Paul, and Jimmy as they appeared in May 1950, in what George describes as "[A] Few of [our] best Family Picture[s]." Photograph was taken in George and Seki's Folsom Street home, where they lived together in Los Angeles between 1946 and 1952. George indicated that he wrote the caption for this photograph in 1960, ten years after taking the picture. Courtesy of the George Nagano Family.

Figure 48. Even though we see Seki standing in the background of this snapshot, George captions his photograph: "one of good Pictures of Mother [at] Paul's home." This photograph appears on an album page labeled "1952 Mother's final year." Courtesy of the George Nagano Family.

Figure 49. In contrast to her husband George, Seki Nagano rarely appeared as the central person in a photograph. In this rare example, Seki is seen in a snapshot captioned by George as "another good Picture of Mother at her home [in] Los Angeles, April 1952." Seki died four months later. Courtesy of the George Nagano Family.

One of the more salient features of George's album is the amount of space and attention given to work. We repeatedly find snapshots of people at work, of work places, of work environments, and a variety of verbal references to work activities. George documents his employment as a laborer—picking lemons in La Canada (north of Los Angeles), as a cantaloupe picker in Watsonville (approximately ninety miles south of San Francisco), and as a trench digger in the Imperial Valley (east of San Diego) (see Figures 50–53). Many of these farm jobs paid one dollar a day.

These were areas where Japanese immigrants had established farming communities before 1920. Again, the historical context, with specific

Figure 50. One of the many places George worked included a migrant labor camp in Westmoreland (approximately 120 miles east of San Diego), California in the Imperial Valley. In a caption talking about himself, George wrote, "Yes! George try out Winemaking, Lemon Picking, Farming, and now Cantaloupe Picking!" Courtesy of the George Nagano Family.

reference to George's work at Watsonville, clarifies this situation. In the recent report, *Five Views—An Ethnic Sites Survey for California,* we read that by 1920,

> *the economic basis of the Japanese community had been firmly established in agriculture and its offshoots—wholesaling, retailing, distributing. The Japanese organized their produce and flower industries vertically, resulting in a system in which all operations were owned and operated by Japanese, from raising the plants to retail sales. This resulted in organizations such as the Southern California Flower Market in Los Angeles, the California Flower Market in San Francisco, Lucky Produce in Sacramento and the City Market in Los Angeles. Cooperatives like Naturipe in Watsonville, Santa Cruz County, were organized to improve the growing, packing and marketing of crops produced by Japanese farmers (Waugh, Yamato, and Okamora 1988: 165).*

George Nagano's employment was closely linked to the emergence

Figure 51. Caption reads: "Imperial Valley Digging Ditches. June 1924." Here we actually see George at work in the fields; pay was about $1.00 per day. These were also areas where Japanese immigrants had established farming communities before 1920. During this period, migrant labor was generally seen as a time of temporary presence, before the development of distinctive and more permanent Japanese American communities. Courtesy of the George Nagano Family.

Figure 52. George's Mexican friends and fellow workers pose in front of crates of cantaloupes at Watsonville Camp, in June 1924. They picked cantaloupes together for about three months. Courtesy of the George Nagano Family.

Figure 53. George worked as a fruit vendor at
a stand owned by Jimmy J. Mura Produce Co.
Courtesy of the George Nagano Family.

Figure 54. On several occasions, George expanded on bibliographic details by including a variety of published materials in his album. Here he inserted a newspaper clipping to describe Seki's former place of employment, "Tokyo's posh Imperial Hotel" (see Figure 7). Courtesy of the George Nagano Family.

of these enterprises. He also worked as a foreman, a winemaker, a produceman, and, later, a church custodian. Under a photograph of the Evergreen Baptist Church, George wrote: "I worked here 1959 to March 1972."

We also learn from this album that Seki worked most of her married life. Traditionally, immigrant Japanese women worked very hard both as wage earners and as providers of parental care for family members. Many of these album photographs are captioned with information relating to Seki's work experiences. For instance, over a newspaper clipping entitled "Tokyo's plush hotel" (see Figure 54) we read: "Seki worked here in 1911 to 1914." Under another picture of Seki, taken in front of the Mayfair Hotel in 1928 (see Figure 55), we read: "Mother worked at a cleaners."[2] And under a portrait of a woman identified as Mrs. Morimoto (see Figure 56), George writes: "I worked at Morimoto['s] store from Sept[ember] 1916 to Feb[ruary] 1917. . . . Seki worked at Methodist Church here 1915–1917." Later in the album, in a caption under a picture of the Nagano family moving to Boyle Heights on August 13, 1933 (see Figure 57), we read: ". . . kind [of] hate to leave dear old home. been here for 11 years—spend many happy and hard days. Dad work[s] at Davis Store. Mother at Asahi Cleaning Shop."

These pictorial and verbal references to work are impressive for several reasons. Hard work has a very meaningful place in both Japanese and Japanese American culture. When anthropologist Akemi Kikumura described the life of her Japanese immigrant mother, she says:

> *Hard work was also a way for Mama to expiate her guilt and a means to ward off self-blame for unfulfilled obligations. In the traditional Japanese sense, hard work was not only a means to achievement and success, but also a means by which an individual could maintain his/ her self-concept as a virtuous person. Working hard and acting in compliance with norms was gratifying because it provided Mama with a way to retain good self-concept despite her "unfilial" deeds (1981: 88).*

In an oral history done in a Japanese American farm community in Del Rey, California, David Mas Masumoto reports the following statement

Figure 55. Seki Nagano posing in front of the Mayfair Hotel in 1928. The Mayfair Hotel was located close to other Japanese boardinghouses adjacent to Little Tokyo, Los Angeles. Manzo Nagano was one of the first Issei to establish a boardinghouse for Japanese workers in North America; George was practicing a trade he may have known through his father's experience. George carefully chronicled their work histories, listing places, type of work, names of employers and fellow employees, and dates—this practice contrasts with Anglo American counterparts which seldom include contexts of employment or work. Courtesy of the George Nagano Family.

Figure 56. Another portrait of one of George Nagano's employers—Mrs. Morimoto, owner of the store where he worked in 1916 and 1917 just before he left Vancouver, British Columbia, for Los Angeles. Courtesy of the George Nagano Family.

made by Mr. G. Oyama, a Nisei: "I swear, my folks planted weeds to make sure I always had more work to keep me busy. You know how Japanese folk are about work, you're only happy and healthy if you're working" (1987: 95). The many photographs of work we found in both Nagano and Uyeda/Miyamura collections may be understood as an extension of this statement. Albums containing such pictures can serve as a means of perpetuating a good self-concept with pictorial signs and evidence of success, achievement and "doing it right."

When we compared the frequency of these work-related photographs to examples found in other picture collections, our results seemed even more impressive. In non-Japanese American albums reviewed for this project, topics related to work and labor are generally ignored, and sometimes never mentioned. In one study, for instance, Richard Oestricher stated:

> People in snapshot albums did not seem to go to work. The world they wanted to remember was the world first of their families, and second of their possessions. Their houses . . . their cars . . . their leisure and its symbols were there. Their work was best forgotten (1981: 56).

Exceptions appear in Anglo American albums from middle-class families when someone owns and/or runs a family business such as a drugstore or a restaurant, or when a family member might be photographed in a work-related uniform, proudly identifying the person as a nurse or a policeman. Album imagery almost always emphasizes the leisure sides of life and strictly ignores the labor side, promoting a labor-leisure dichotomy.

George's photographic attention to work is all the more exceptional since some of his work experiences, such as the migrant labor examples, depicted in George's album, could not have been pleasureable. While George does make reference to the "hard days," the images do not show any of the difficult times. An incompatability exists between George's written and the visual expressions. These pictures represent an attempt to make the best of difficult circumstances. It is clear that preserving a recognition of these work experiences and maintaining an identification with fellow workers were very significant.

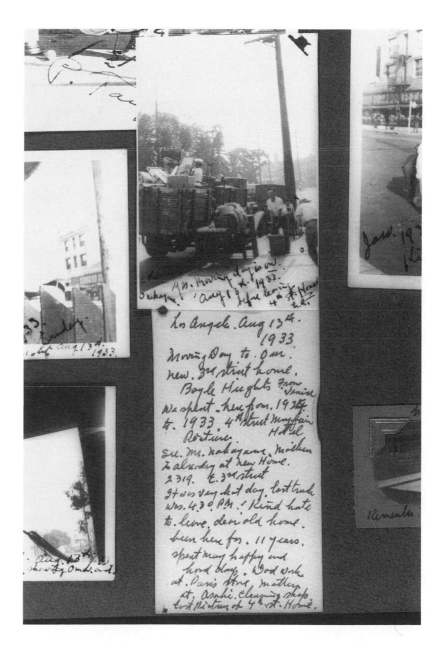

Figure 57. Snapshot of the Nagano family packing their possessions on August 13, 1933 as they move from Venice to what they referred to as their "3rd Street home" (2319 East 3rd Street) in Boyle Heights, East Los Angeles. In addition to mentioning work in George's amended caption ("Yes, Moving day is *on*"), this photograph represents a variation on the "last time" theme mentioned earlier. Courtesy of the George Nagano Family.

Figure 58. Formal portrait of the membership of the Vancouver Methodist Church made by the Saito Studios in December 1916. Seki and Tyrus Nagano are seated second from the left in the front row. George labels this photograph "A Farewell Picture with member[s] of the Church on Powell Street," and as "Rev. Matsunaga['s] farewell . . . Also, Mother's (Seki's) farewell picture. Left for U.S.A. this year, 1917." Seki worked at Reverend Matsunaga's home—the Nagano family pastor—between 1914 and 1917. George later amended his first caption, adding that "Seki worked here . . . helped cooking breakfast and dinner at church." Churches played several important roles for Japanese immigrants, including language learning, social gatherings, and employment opportunities. Courtesy of the George Nagano Family.

Another striking characteristic of George Nagano's album is the attention given to churches and religious matters. In other albums studied before this project, these topics appeared to be restricted to direct associations with a wedding, a confirmation, a holy communion, or a christening; pictures of the family priest or family pastor may appear in albums (or even wallets) of religious families. Otherwise, church-related imagery is rare.

However, George included a considerable number of snapshot photographs of churches and church-related activities. We have already referred to several relevant examples, including the photograph of the Evergreen Baptist Church, and views of Methodist and Baptist church groups (see Figures 58 and 59). George's written comments refer to church-going occasions. In two examples (see Figures 60 and 61), we read:

Sunday July 7th 1968. On our way to Church [–] Junko

Figure 59. We see that George continued taking and saving photographs of his church memberships, including this portrait captioned: "Easter Sunday April 10—1951 Issei Baptist Church." George was careful to point to where "Mother" (Seki) was standing in the congregation. Courtesy of the George Nagano Family.

George Mrs Kuno. Issei Baptist Church. Tyrus goes to Nisei Church. Member of long standing since 1946.

Sunday May 20th 1965   To Church to-day Junko to Issei Church and Tyrus to Nisei Church   Both Baptist.

And under a photograph of what appears initially to be only a street corner, George writes: "Evergreen Playground and Issei and Nisei Church where Seki use[d] to go every Sunday."

The representation of churches is closely related to the Nagano family's participation and identity in the Japanese American community. This affiliation appears to date from George and Seki's association with the Methodist Church in Vancouver, and continues with their participation in the Union Church in Little Tokyo and the Evergreen Baptist Church in Boyle Heights. George's son, "Reverend Paul" Nagano, was well known and highly respected in the Los Angeles Japanese

Figure 60. In a snapshot taken by Tyrus Nagano in July 1968, we see (left to right) Junko Nagano Morisaku, George Nagano, and close family friend Mrs. Kuno "on our way to [Issei Baptist] church." The Nagano family shifted their allegiance to Baptist churches when they settled in Los Angeles—a pattern not unfamiliar to first generation Japanese Americans. Courtesy of the George Nagano Family.

American community as the pastor of the Evergreen Baptist Church.

Historically, the church played, and continues to play, a very important part in Japanese American family life. Churches, whether Christian, Buddhist, or Shinto, were the focus of activity for most Japanese communities, and were often the earliest organizations to be established (Waugh, Yamoto, and Okamura 1988: 168). Los Angeles is an important location in this regard. Modell, for instance, notes that at first white missionaries were instrumental in organizing religious life of the Japanese Americans in Los Angeles: "These missionaries were the first and ultimately the most faithful white friends the Japanese Americans had" (1977: 75). He also noted that Caucasian Christians sought to win over Japanese immigrants before the Buddhists tried to do so, and by 1910, five Christian missions served the Los Angeles Japanese American community (1977: 76).

Many authors have been quick to note that churches provided both "religious sustenance" and social life. In addition to providing the symbolic support associated with ceremonial life—for example, regular services, weddings, funerals, and special services for religious holidays—churches provided places for both youth groups and women's organizations, recreation facilities, and information on employment opportunities. Modell uses the example of the Union Church in Los Angeles (photographs of the Union Church were found in the Nagano materials) as a focal point of community activities, "including many of the 'social church' variety" (1977: 77).

In addition to these socially integrative functions, the early presence of churches takes on significance as a factor of adaptation to American society and culture. Kitano (1976) adds many insights on how Christian churches functioned as an agent of acculturation, especially for women. Acculturative features of album representation will be discussed further in Chapter Five.

We are locating the Nagano family photograph collection within this historical context, within the regional characteristics of a large urban population on the West Coast, and within a community where Reverend Paul Nagano was so well known. It is not surprising that we

Figure 61. Another church-related snapshot taken by George Nagano on Sunday, May 20, 1965, showing his daughter Junko Nagano Morisaku and his eldest son, Tyrus Nagano. Courtesy of the George Nagano Family.

Figure 62. This is a 1968 advertisement for the Bon festival at one of the main temples in Japan Town, located in downtown Los Angeles. The O in OBON is an honorary prefix. In Japan, Bon is one of the most important seasonal rites held to attend to the ancestors, comparable to the Christian "All Souls Day." In Hawaii and the mainland U.S., Japanese American Bon celebrations include both public and private community activities. In its Japanese American context, Bon has shifted away from actually communing with the dead to honoring the dead and celebrating summer. George documented the carnivals of the most important Buddhist churches in Japan Town—important community events that he attended—even though he was a devout Christian (see Smith 1974: 99; De Francis 1973: 45–46). Courtesy of the George Nagano Family.

find references to churches and church-related activities in this Japanese American album. Family albums such as "Nagano's Mother 1910–1952" offer interesting insights and neglected evidence of what different groups of immigrants do with their religious beliefs, commitments, and church affiliations as they make subtle adjustments, accommodations, and transitions from one geographic region of the world to another.

One other reference to religious matters will serve as a connection to our next topic, namely attention to death. George's album contains repeated reference, in both pictures and captions, to "Bon" (see Figures 62 and 63). In Japan, Bon is understood as a popular Buddhist holy day, and is celebrated between the thirteenth and fifteenth of August. Known as the Festival of the Dead, this time is devoted to ancestor worship and requital of the souls of the dead (Smith 1974: 99). Smith notes: "Bon is by far the most elaborate of the four seasonal rites directed to the collectivity of the ancestors" (1974: 99). The Bon festival remains as one of the most important festivals in Japanese American communities (DeFrancis 1973: 45). Discussion of how Bon is related to themes of

Figure 63. George's caption reads: "Koyosan Buddhist Church OBON Carnival, Sunday, June 23, 1968." The Koyosan church, located a half-block from the Nishi Hongwanji Buddhist Temple (see Figure 62), is recognized as an important temple and community center in Japan Town. George photographed the Awa Odori folk dancers from Japan performing traditional Bon dances. At that time, street folk dancing was performed in addition to the traditional rites at the temple and in the home. Most temples have added a church carnival modeled after American church bazaars with food booths and craft sales. In this 1968 example, George noted "this is a big crowd." Courtesy of the George Nagano family.

acculturation, *ie,* and belonging will appear in Chapter Five. But George Nagano's references to Bon take us from a focus on religion to the theme of death.

We find that George gives significant pictorial attention to the death of a family member. Although the topic might be simply considered 'death' in a Western sense, the reference for the Issei would be the *ie* —the concept of the family unit as an unbroken continuum which includes the ancestors, living family members, and future generations. Funeral rites and care of family graves, as forms of ancestor worship, were traditionally the responsibility of the head of household. Evidence that George took this responsibility very seriously appears in his album. Examples are found on the pages devoted to 1952, the year of Seki's death (see Figure 30). Explicit references to Seki's funeral include (see Figures 64 and 65): "Evergreen Cemetery Aug[ust] 20th 1952. Our dear Mother['s] Funeral. Passed away on Aug[ust] 13th Wednesday 4:30 PM at Japanese Hospital. She just went away very Peacefully." On the following page, we see a kind of group picture of the people attending Seki's funeral—a type of photograph we found in several other Japanese American albums studied for this project (see Figure 66). For many Japanese immigrants, this kind of photograph served as important documentary evidence to be sent to family members in Japan, demonstrating that the deceased had been given a proper funeral. In one of George's captions we read: "Mothers Funeral. Aug[ust] 20 1952. All of Mother['s] friend[s] are here, some from far away place[s]. Mother will be happy in her home in Heaven, resting Peacefully."

Several authors have noted that fumerals were "one of the primary functions of the Buddhist church in America, reinforcing Japanese values of collectivity (family and community) and ancestor worship" (Lukes and Okihiro 1985: 97). This is not to say that Buddhist and Christian religions or funeral services were the same; there were some similarities and dissimilarities. By knowing that Seki's funeral was a Christian service, we have an interesting example of adaptation and transformation—a Japanese American expression of Japanese values and behavior.

George also documents his visits to Seki's gravesite on the same page

Figure 64. Seven photographs carefully placed and captioned on page 73 of George Nagano's album entitled "Nagano's Mother 1910–1952" in the section devoted to "1952 Mother's Final Year." The top three photographs were taken at Seki's grave in the Evergreen Cemetery; the center photograph depicts Seki's funeral; of the bottom three, two were taken during the Christmas after Seki's death. Courtesy of the George Nagano Family.

Figure 65. "Our dear Mother['s] Funeral." Color snapshot taken at Seki's gravesite in Evergreen Cemetery during her funeral on August 20, 1952. These snapshots are not commonly found in Anglo American albums; their frequency in Japanese and Japanese American albums indicates a culturally different way of conceptualizing death and remembering the funerals of family members. Courtesy of the George Nagano Family.

Figure 66. "Mothers Funeral." An important color snapshot because it indicates how many people honored Seki and the Nagano family at the time of her death. George writes: "All of Mother['s] friend[s] are here, come from far away place[s]." Courtesy of the George Nagano Family.

Figure 67. Other examples of death-related imagery include scenes of people visiting the graves of family members on such holidays as Easter, Memorial Day, and Mother's Day. Here George is seen kneeling by flowers placed in front of Seki's gravestone in Evergreen Cemetery. Courtesy of the George Nagano Family.

Figure 68. "Memorial Day, May 30, 1968." George used the self-timer on his camera to take this snapshot of himself. Caption reads: "Just 16 years ago since you gone Mother. We all miss you. Junko, Tyrus, Jack and Paul." Courtesy of the George Nagano Family.

(see Figures 67 and 68). We see three snapshots of the Nagano grave-marker. Under one photograph (see Figure 69), we read: "1st picture before the grave stone. rather empty now but by 1960 began to [be] crowded here." Again, we find George reporting changes in ways that could be notes to himself or to his sons.

Similar illustrations are found on pages that George added to his original version of the album. For instance, in a photograph dated May 1973, we see Tyrus, George's first-born son, standing next to Seki's grave marker, and under a photograph dated Sunday, May 11, 1975 (see Figure 70), we read: "Mother['s] Day. George, Junko at Mother['s] grave. Evergreen Cemetery. Mother['s] grave is crowded these days. all Japanese here."

Thus, in George's album, we find symbolic representation coinciding with Japanese behavioral patterns and values. This Japanese American album gives straightforward evidence of the persistence of Japanese customs related to the caring for graves of deceased relatives and maintaining the Japanese concept of family or *ie*. George's references to the care of Seki's grave are clear messages. On page 71 of this album, we find George directing his sons as follows: "1952 Mothers final year. . . . We all miss her, do not forget to visit her grave, boys. Wonderful Mother to us all—Dad 10/14/1960." Sons must fulfill their family's obligations by visiting the graves of their parents. It was, in any case, an important value that George instructed his sons not to forget.

The literature on Japanese culture mentions the common use of photographs in association with either funerals or remembering deceased members of a family. Robert Smith offers the following observations that integrate interests in photographs, funerals, altars, and generational continuity:

> *Another issue linking the living and the dead is that of the portrait of the deceased, now universally found at funerals and the early memorial services. A priest told us that it is very difficult to find just the right photograph for use in the altar. When the elderly grandfather of a family in Chutiku was killed on the highway, his family found that the only suitable picture they had of him was one that I had taken in 1951. They remarked that they never did find a good one of his wife.*

Figure 69. A few days after the funeral, George had this snapshot taken of himself as he stood next to Seki's grave, before the gravestone was in place. Similar compositions and content are found in this album for 1954, 1968, 1973, 1975. Courtesy of the George Nagano Family.

Handwritten on photograph:
*Sunday May 11 - 1975
Mother Day George Junko at mother
grave, Evergreen Cemetery, mother
grave is crowded Thursday, all Japanese.
here 54 yrs ... Junk 12y, Tyrus.*

Figure 70. George Nagano and Junko Nagano Morisaku on each side of Seki Nagano's gravestone. This color snapshot was taken by Tyrus Nagano in the Evergreen Cemetery on Mother's Day, May 11, 1975. Courtesy of the George Nagano Family.

. . . An acquaintance remarked to me that his family had been unable to locate an appropriate picture of his mother, "She died at seventy-five, and all the good pictures of her were taken when she was much younger. You had better take a good one of me while you are here!" The problem has not escaped the attention of a professional photographer in Shionoe. The glass-covered display case in front of his shop shows two examples of what can be done to salvage the situation. On display are two snapshots, one of a man and one of a woman, both wearing everyday clothing and standing against some ordinary, everyday background. From these snapshots the photographer has made two large funerary portraits, with backgrounds wiped clean and garments transformed into formal black kimono (1978: 157–58).[3]

Another example of funeral-related photography comes from a 1984 study of Japanese families temporarily living in Houston, Texas. Sociologist Lynn Blinn described a case when a funeral director hired a professional photographer to take a formal picture of a woman holding the urn of her husband's ashes while her son-in-law held a photograph of the man. Blinn added that the picture of the deceased had

been draped in black and white ribbons and the remaining family members dressed in black. The wife selected the picture of the deceased that she wished to have enlarged to life size and used for this occasion. The son-in-law was selected to hold the picture in keeping with the custom of "muko yooshi" or adopting a daughter's husband as a son and successor to the headship of the family. On the anniversary of the death or "meinichi" this group picture as well as the picture of the deceased will be viewed in memorium (1986: 19).[4]

In Japan, it is common to find portrait photographs placed in a household altar. Dishes are prepared or flowers are gathered, according to the preferences of the departed, and offered at the family altar. In these examples, photographs are used to "heighten the effect" of visualizing the departed. Several references to this practice were found in the literature; two come from Robert Smith's fieldwork in Japan:

> *In one house the family was observing the "first bon" (hatsubon) for*
> *the spirit of its grandmother, who had died within the year. . . . In the*
> *alcove beside the altar were two large photographs of the deceased and*
> *her husband, who had died some years before (1978: 163).*
> *In the altar of a family of his acquaintance there are photographs of*
> *two deceased daughters of the house. Both were Catholic nuns and are*
> *shown in their habits. Their father had felt that it would be inappropri-*
> *ate either to have Buddhist tablets made for them or to abandon them*
> *altogether. The photographs are his compromise (1974: 140).*

Given these cultural details of Japanese practices associated with photographs, it is less surprising to find funeral-related pictures in a Japanese American family album.[5]

A fourth characteristic of George's album involves his pictorial recognition of last-time events. George's album contains an interesting variety of "farewell pictures." Captioned information often refers to the last time someone or something was photographed or seen, or the last time a specific event took place. Examples of photographs that are explicitly labeled "Farewell Pictures" include church portraits (see Figure 58) and snapshots taken before leaving for the Poston Relocation Camp in 1942 (see Figure 71). At that time, local police and the FBI were under orders to confiscate cameras from all Japanese Americans before their evacuation to relocation camps. Cameras were classified as contraband materials. This must have added to the personal meaning and historical significance of last-time pictures taken at this time. Similar "just-before-leaving-for-camp" shots were found in two albums made by Japanese American families who relocated to Seabrook, New Jersey, after internment.

We also found a "Farewell Picture [taken] at Poston, Arizona" before George and Seki left for St. Paul, Minnesota in 1943" (see Figure 72). While in the camps, government officials made cameras available through block managers; they could be borrowed for taking pictures during special occasions such as weddings, new babies, sons leaving for military duty, etc. As time passed, cameras became more plentiful as some were smuggled into the camps and some were even purchased through mail-order catalogs.

Figure 71. George captions this snapshot as follows: "Farewell Picture. [We] depart to different Relocation Centers, April 1942. Hollenbeck Park. Some to Manzanar Center, some gone to Heart Mountain, some to Poston, Arizona." Courtesy of the George Nagano Family.

Figure 72. In addition to pictures devoted to "leaving for camp," George's album included "leaving camp—farewell photographs." One example shows Tyrus, Seki, and George posing for a snapshot just before they left Poston, Arizona, for St. Paul, Minnesota in November 1943. To avert and diffuse any sense of continued potential threat, the government did not permit evacuees to resettle on the West Coast. Those who returned to locations in the Western Defense Zone and were caught were sentenced to long jail terms. (Courtesy of George Nagano Family)

Wishing you a merry Xmas and Happy New Year. 1921. From. George.

Farewell to Victoria. Jan. 1922

Figure 73. Farewells to places, cities, homes, and even events are acknowledged in George's album. Here, on a postcard used as a Christmas card ("Wishing you a merry Xmas and Happy New Year. 1921") George writes: "Farewell to Victoria, Jan[uary] 1922." Courtesy of the George Nagano Family.

In other examples, George was fond of labeling the significance of a particular image for its farewell or last-time qualities. Examples are found in such captions as "Farewell to Victoria. Jan[uary] 1922" (see Figure 73) and written under a snapshot taken at a Japanese picnic (see Figure 74): "This was our last get together at Venice [Ca.]." In a related example (see Figure 75), we read: "July 1923. Venice Japanese Group Picnic. Seki in races. [We] enjoyed big day. Our last Picnic as we like to move to Los Angeles soon." Later, on album page 25, we read: "Sayonara This year 1924 was last time we live[d] in Ocean Park, Cal[ifornia] . . . ," written under a snapshot of Paul (Makoto) and two neighbor boys, (see Figure 76). Pictures like these might best be classified as "sayonara snapshots." In another Japanese American album, I found several pictures taken during a "sayonara party."[6]

This last-view or last-look perspective also applies to a sequence of the Nagano homes. Under a snapshot of George and Seki's 4th Street

Figure 74. This last time focused on a "last get-together" during a Japanese picnic, while the Naganos lived in Venice, California. George adds: "In July 1921 George['s] family went to Venice [for] Japanese Picnic [to] meet some old friends." Courtesy of the George Nagano Family.

Figure 75. Snapshot showing (left to right) Tyrus, Paul, and Jack Nagano captioned: "One Sunday morning at Beach Ocean Park July 1923" during a Japanese picnic—"our last picnic" before leaving for Los Angeles. Courtesy of the George Nagano Family.

Figure 76. Example of "Sayonara" photograph taken on a Sunday morning in March 1924, and originally captioned by George as "Last Picture with Paul's friend in Venice, Ocean Park Home March 1924." Courtesy of the George Nagano Family.

Figure 77. George Nagano took this color snapshot during the Pasadena Rose Parade on Wednesday, January 1, 1969. Beginning in 1919, George was a spectator at the Rose Bowl Parade every year; he often documented this event, and parades became a consistent topic in George's album. The caption here once again cites the significance of "Yes, my last time." Courtesy of the George Nagano Family.

house, we read: "last picture from E[ast] 4th St[reet], Aug[ust] 13th/ 33." And groups of people are given the same treatment; under a picture of four men taken in 1941, we read: "One of four last Pictures together Jan[uary] 1941."

The recognition of George's own last appearance at important and favorite events appears in several captions. Under a snapshot taken on New Year's Day, 1969 (see Figure 77), we read: "My last time at Pasadena Rose Parade. First time in year 1919. . . . From 1970 [on] I watch [it] on TV each year."

The significance of last times even applies to animals such as their family pets. Under a picture of their dog (see Figure 78), we read: ". . . Good old Tommy [—] Last picture 1941 Los Angeles. . . . Tommy died Nov[ember] 15th 1941." And later under a picture taken after Seki died in 1952 (see Figure 79), we read: "Mother['s] last chicken Oct[ober] 11—1954."

We found a survival of this habit into the Yonsei generation, in an album made by one of George's grandsons, Steve Nagano. Documenting a trip with his friends to Hawaii, Steve began this album with snapshots taken during a farewell party in San Francisco. Later in the same album, we found other pictures of another farewell when Steve's friends had to return to San Francisco. Reminiscent of George's annotations, we read the caption, "we miss you all."

In many non-Japanese American albums, the *beginnings* of events, activities, lives of people, or pieces of material culture are given much more attention than ends or terminations. For instance, snapshot collections and albums are full of photographs that record and, indeed, celebrate such events as a baby's first tooth, first steps, a child's first birthday, first trip to the beach, first snowstorm, first day going to school. Sometimes the picture record includes shots of the first bicycle, first car, first date, and so on. While we could argue that commencement and graduation pictures show the last time that all of these people will be gathered together in the same place, the point is that most album-makers do not attend to this characteristic of the photographed event; that perspective is seemingly not relevant to the album's interpretation of life. The significance of "we made it" or "proud to graduate" overrides the recognition of "last time together."

Figure 78. Ground-level snapshot of the Nagano's pet dog "Tommy." Even the family pet is accorded a kind of farewell or last time attention as George writes, "Good old Tommy last Picture . . . Tommy died Nov. 15th 1941." Courtesy of the George Nagano Family.

George's notes and pictures may be linked to the Japanese custom of demarcating endings. Clapping will be used to signal the end of a Kabuki play or the close of the Tokyo stock market at the end of the year. The conclusion of some event is often symbolized by a knot or tie, a *musubi*. It represents both tying together loose ends as a conclusion as well as symbolizing a new beginning—uniting the two to make one. Some examples are the *en-musubi* joining two people in marriage or the words for son, *musuko*, and daughter, *musume*, derived from the stem *musubi* (Condon and Kurata 1974).

Maintaining Ie *as the Communication of Unity*

The two main sections of this chapter—one concentrating on form, the other on content—are held together by an integrated theory of culture and communication. Patterns of communication demonstrated by George's use of his camera and album are intimately tied to *ie* as a cornerstone notion of both Japanese and Japanese American culture.

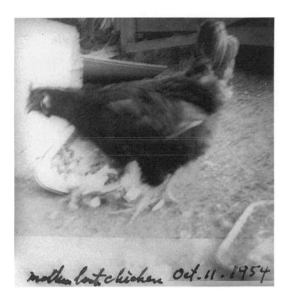

Figure 79. Just after the pages devoted to Seki's death in 1952, George included this snapshot captioned: "Mother's last chicken Oct. 11 - 1954." He also included snapshots of Seki's favorite chickens; under one, George wrote: "Mother['s] chicken. She['s] not there to feed [them] any more." Courtesy of the George Nagano Family.

We have discovered visual representations that both demonstrate and illustrate how communicative message forms can be used in the transmission and indeed transformation of culture. The ritualized behaviors we have seen involving altars, gravesites, bon activities, "ohaka-mairi" and "obustudan" practices can all be tied into a theme of belonging. In these ways the Issei were passing on important cultural ideas regarding identity, kinship, and community. The notion of *ie* is featured in this chapter, and the importance of belonging will be elaborated in Chapter Five.

The four topics that we found highlighted in George Nagano's album are held together by a theme that relates Japanese and Japanese American culture—namely the communication of unity and its relation to *ie*. In anthropologist Takie Lebra's book, *Japanese Patterns of Behavior*, she discusses this theme as follows:

> *Intimate behavior is first characterized by expression and confirmation of unity, oneness, or solidarity, based on mutual liking and emotional attachment. . . . Unity is communicated outwardly and inwardly. The outward communication of unity typically takes the form of play and enjoyment—doing pleasurable things together. Small wonder that Japanese go in for group participation. . . . "Doing things together" necessitates "being together," occupying the same space (1976: 115).*

We saw how a concern with "doing things together" was emphasized in contexts of work and church groups. We found a similar pattern of attention to George's sports teams. But most of all, George was relating this theme of unity to maintaining a sense of family, household, or *ie* as previously mentioned. Several authors have emphasized the centrality of this notion. For instance, anthropologist John W. Connor describes *ie* as follows:

> *This basic sociological unit of co-residential members of a house is called* ie *in Japanese. The term* ie *is often used in sociological literature as an equivalent of family, but the English term household is close to the conception since it includes all co-residents and is not necessarily restricted only to the members of a family. . . . Further, the* ie *is not*

simply a contemporary household as its English counterpart suggests, but is conceptualized in the time continuum from past to future, including not only the actual residential members but also dead members, with some projection also towards those yet unborn. The ie *is always conceived as persisting through time by the succession of the members (Nakane 1967: 2–3, as found in Connor 1977: 22).*

There appears to be general agreement that the *ie* has changed in contemporary times owing to forces of increased modernization and urbanization. However, Nakane believes "the concept of this traditional household institution, *ie,* still persists in the various group identities which are termed *uchi,* a colloquial form of *ie*" (1970: 7). Nakane cites examples of company and union organizations among other groups as ways of tying people together in recognizable, identifiable groups. Many Japanese American examples will be presented throughout several chapters.

However, is it legitimate to imply that this concept is relevant to Japanese American culture? While there appears to be some debate on this issue, Connor argues that the Issei brought the *ie* ideal with them, and "it would seem reasonable to expect that they would attempt to preserve as much as possible of the *ie* ideal as they could in a new country" (1977: 28). Connor continues his argument as follows:

While the evidence for the preservation of the ie *ideal is indirect, it is nonetheless quite strong. . . . This is not to say that the Issei were completely successful. . . . Unquestionably, they realized that they were not in Japan and that adaptations had to be made. Nevertheless, . . . it must also be said . . . that they also succeeded in passing at least a feeling for the* ie *concept to their children and even to their grandchildren (Connor 1977: 296–97).*

Given the emphasis on household, and these comments on attention to past and future, would not the family album be an ideal vehicle to accomplish some of these objectives and functions? George's use of his photographs accompanied by his written comments plays an important role in providing a sense of unity to the *ie.* He sought to keep Seki informed of family matters while he transmitted important values to the succeeding generations. We have seen how he used his album as a way to communicate an integration of the past, present, and future.

We chose to discuss the communicative value of this album and to highlight some specific features of its content and construction. It is suggested that these choices of pictorial content are intimately linked to traditional Japanese values of the Meiji/Tokugawa era and to the emergence of a Japanese American value scheme. A family album both reflects and expresses cultural values, and, in turn, helps build a sense of continuity in the face of dramatic individual, social, and cultural change. Later we will seek a better understanding of what people accomplish psychologically, socially, and culturally by organizing elaborate versions of their lives in the format of photograph albums. A statement by made by George's grandson, Steve Nagano, provides a nice summary at this point:

> *George's album serves as the cord that ties these [extended] families together. . . . Albums like these provide us with links to the past, rich with experiences. There is within many families someone like George who takes the time to remember, record, and share the frozen moments in the past, giving continuity and understanding to future generations. It is these personal histories, however shared, that bring life to the history of struggle and determination of Japanese in America.*

Chapter Four

The Uyeda/Miyamura Photograph Collection

In Chapter Three, we discussed what one Japanese American man did in making his family album. By examining George Nagano's album, we were able to show how a family album functions as a highly selective and well-integrated collection of visual and verbal forms of communication. We've also begun to discuss how both image content and use can be linked to the Japanese American interpretation of "Japanese" tradition.

In our second case study, we take a broader view—examining how several Japanese Americans shot photographs, made albums, and used their pictures within an extended family and over several generations. Our study of the Uyeda/Miyamura family focuses on alternative forms of pictorial expression—how family members have displayed, exchanged, distributed, and stored their personal photographs.

The Uyeda/Miyamura family provided us with an interesting case study because of the volume of their photographic records and the various ways they used their pictures. This collection documents more than seven decades of their family life in Gallup, New Mexico. We sought to learn more about how the social context of Gallup contributed to the Uyeda/Miyamura's use of personal photographs. From the beginning, we wanted to discover how the Uyeda/Miyamura photographic record might reflect social circumstances of life in Gallup, and how this view would differ from what we found in Los Angeles. But, even within this diversity, we found a continuity in pictorial content, personal information, and cultural expression linked to Japanese American life across generations. We sought (1) a more comprehensive understanding of how the Uyeda/Miyamura photographs recorded the unique characteristics of an immigrant family settling in a small western town, and (2) some indication of the ways that Japanese traditions persisted in this model of pictorial representation.

This second point is even more significant when we recognize the many changes that have taken place in Gallup's Japanese American community over the years. Within the Uyeda/Miyamura family, there has been a lot of dispersal and relocating of the Nisei siblings. For instance, Michiko and Momoko left their Gallup home to attend the Barnes Business School in Denver, Colorado (Colorado was one of the few western states that did not overtly discourage Japanese Americans from settling). As of this writing, two siblings have remained in Gallup (Michiko and Hershey), while four others are in living in the greater Los Angeles area. Being raised in the Southwest has given the Miyamura and Uyeda Niseis a different interpretation of their Japanese past, whether they currently reside in Los Angeles or Gallup. Our analysis, however, focuses on photographic materials from the Gallup area.

Identifying the Family Photographers

Although we were able to acquire adequate information on the family history, it was much more difficult to obtain details about the family photographers who are no longer living. We have relied on personal interviews with family members who volunteered information on the photographic habits of both Frank Uyeda and Yaichi Miyamura. For instance, we learned that Yaichi kept a daily diary. But family members were not able to locate it, and some considered it lost. When Michiko talked about diary-keeping and her father, Yaichi, she said:

> *I don't know who has his diary, though. But he wrote what he did everyday. And he says, "I played cards today and I lost." He says, "I had to wash my socks, so I didn't have enough money to go eat." I mean, he had a diary, he kept a diary on whatever. . . . It's probably lost . . . and I think [maybe] Shigeko has it.*

Here we find another similarity between Yaichi Miyamura and George Nagano; but as mentioned previously, diary-writing and other forms of detailed documentation are familiar Japanese traits and are found with some regularity among Issei and Nisei.

Frank Uyeda was the first member of the Uyeda family to become interested in keeping a detailed photographic record of his life. When Frank returned to Gallup in 1915, after a six-year period of education in Japan, he was using his own camera. As Frank's wife, Grace Uyeda, said: "Yeah he [Frank] had different kinds [of cameras], movie, and gee, Japanese-made cameras, and he has those cameras like the double front views [twin lens camera]. He used to love to take pictures." Frank owned a Brownie box camera and had access to printing and enlarging equipment. We learned that Frank processed and printed his own pictures; he frequently made several prints from the same negative and enlarged selected portions of an image for special purposes. We also discovered that by 1925, Frank owned and used a much more sophisticated camera—a Graflex (see Figure 80); and by 1941 he was using a 35mm camera as well as a motion-picture camera. However, Frank Uyeda's cameras were confiscated during World War II and could not be reclaimed—they had been "lost" according to authorities. After the war, he bought an entire new set of cameras and continued to take pictures as he had before, for his family and for the Japanese American community.

Frank was considered the "semiofficial" community photographer. Family members often referred to him as the earliest and most prolific photographer among them. We learned more about Frank's role as a photographer from one of Chiko Miyamura Herrera's albums in which she chronicled the Miyamura family. This album contained numerous photographs, or copies of photographs, that Frank took and then developed for members of the Japanese American community. The same album contained large photographs of Japanese American picnics from the 1930s and 1963, a series of large photographs of the celebration of the Emperor's Birthday at the Nippon Gakuen, the Japanese School (c.1930), and numerous photographs taken by Frank of the Uyeda/ Miyamura family.

Figure 80. Snapshot of Frank Uyeda posed with his Graflex camera and his dog (c. 1925) with landscape of the New Mexico hills near Gallup seen in the background. Courtesy of the Grace Tomoko Uyeda Family.

Figure 81. Extended family portrait taken by Frank Uyeda during their annual "Picnic July 1963," in which he carefully selected only family members for the shot. Chiko is seen kneeling on the left, front row, and Grace Uyeda is seated next to her; Chiko's children, Nancy Herrera Ortiz and Michael Herrera, are seated in the front row on the far left; and Frank's uncle, Yaichi, is standing directly behind Michael. (All other people are listed in the text.) Courtesy of the Chiko Miyamura Herrera Family.

Frank photographed a large group of people at the annual Japanese American picnic held in July 1963 (see Figure 81). Although there were many other Japanese American families at the picnic, only Frank's relatives make up the group appearing in the photograph. Chiko Miyamura Herrera remembered how the picture was taken: "this was *just* our group. . . . Frank wanted to take a picture of the whole bunch." It would seem that Frank included all the families present who were descended from his father, Heizo Uyeda, and his uncle (father's brother), Yaichi Miyamura—including Frank's nieces and nephews (children of his sister, Kika Uyeda Taira) as well as grandchildren (see kinship diagram in Appendix B for a clearer idea of these relationships). As Chiko explained:

> *This is the Tairas, the Uyedas and the Miyamuras . . . Keiko Taira, Chiko Herrera carrying Tori Ortiz, Tomoko-san carrying Sissy, . . .*

Figures 82, 83, and 84. Three self-portrait snapshots photographed, developed, and printed by Yaichi Miyamura at his restaurant, the Lucky Lunch, c. 1950. Courtesy of the Chiko Miyamura Herrera Family.

Taira, Terry and Kelly Miyamura, Nancy Ortiz, "Butch" (Alex Jr.) Ortiz, Alex Ortiz, Michael Herrera, Nancy Herrera, Kevin Taira, Laura Kimura, Mary Kimura, Kika Taira (Kika-san), Yoshiko-san carrying Alicia Alayne Taira, Pat Miyamura, Cynthia Uyeda, Mike Miyamura, Ronny Tanakawa (Suzi Miyamura Tanakawa's son on vacation in Gallup), Gerry Herrera, Yaichi Miyamura, Johnny Herrera, Johnny Kauzlarich, Wilma Taira, Johnny Jr. Herrera, Alex Ortiz, and Mark Uyeda.

As in the Nagano materials, we find another picture that celebrates family unity, and one that illustrates themes of belonging and the communication of unity.

Yaichi Miyamura is the second of our featured family photographers. We learned that Yaichi became interested in photography through his nephew, Frank Uyeda. Yaichi began taking, processing, and printing photographs as a hobby. He experimented with poses similar to studio shots, and, like Frank, he made cropped copy photos from older photographs (see Figures 82, 83, and 84). Most of Yaichi's photographs were made for his children. He apparently shot and developed many photographs of his grandchildren for his children. Yaichi's daughter, Chiko, remembered: "Either my Dad was taking them [pictures] or Frank was taking them and we did have a little Brownie. I remember . . . that's what I used to take to high school was a little Brownie Box." And Michiko, Yaichi's third daughter, remembered: "Easter and Christmas and all that—those are the times when they would take pictures." But it was Yaichi and Tori's first son, Hershey Miyamura, who recalled other details:

I think my father really got into photography when Mike [Hershey's first son] was born [1954]—he was experimenting a little with it before that [but] not too much. . . . He had all the equipment—darkroom, enlarger. . . . He must have read and studied off and on after work hours. That often made me wonder how he ever learned to do it on his own—he's quite a guy. . . . He didn't do too much of enlarging and things, but once that Mike was born, I noticed that he started taking more and more pictures, and every time we had another child, he'd take all kinds of pictures and enlarge them.

Chiko also related stories of Yaichi making motion pictures—home movies which included the wedding of his granddaughter Nancy Herrera to Alex Ortiz. Hershey added: "His home movies were all taken between the early '50s and late '60s. . . . I have several rolls he's taken . . . a lot of the Rose Bowl and Indian Ceremonials . . . [and] of the children growing up. He just did it for his own enjoyment."

To this date, we have not been able to locate any albums that Yaichi may have put together, but we have found many of his individual photographs. Most of these pictures are in Chiko's album. We discovered that Yaichi's selection of topics coincided with some of the patterned choices made by George Nagano—a selection described in Chapter Three. But both differences and similarities play roles in the development of our analysis and conclusions.

Patterns of Image Use: Exchange and Sharing

The significance of Frank's and Yaichi's photography is understood better when we explore what family members did with their photographs and what they continue to do with new pictures they now make on their own initiatives. When we examined the photograph collections kept by both Uyeda and Miyamura family members, we discovered many identical pictures—photographs that had originally been taken by Frank or Yaichi. These photographs had been duplicated and distributed to individual members of both families.

We have also learned that the role of photographer seems to be shared by all of Yaichi's Nisei children. They have been taking and exchanging photographs since daughters Michiko and Momoko left home. Michiko Miyamura Yoshida remarked: "My sister (Momoko) and I were the only ones that left home early to go to school. I mean we were the only ones to leave and naturally, being away from home, we always received pictures; they would send us pictures." The exchange of photographs continued. As the Miyamura brothers and sisters married and formed families, photographs of newborn children would be mailed or given in person to family members. Chiko explained: "I think it was more because of the children when they were babies . . . they [the parents] want to send you a picture of the baby. So they used to take studio pictures and mail them out."

This experience should sound very familiar to readers who have made family photographs. This activity is widespread and not particularly characteristic of Japanese or Japanese American families. But we are provided with an explicit example of how people use their photographs as a form of interpersonal and family communication. We know from other sources and examples that this kind of interfamily communication is extremely important to Japanese immigrant families. Here an important social function of family photography is illustrated and demonstrated to be a part of everyday life. Pictures were distributed to introduce new family members and to incorporate newborn children into the extended family. People not only learn of the existence of new family members, they are actually treated to views of new people. Networks of communication are maintained and reified, and photographs are used to enhance the quality of communication between family members. We were very impressed with the regularity, frequency, and quantity of photographic exchanges that took place over several generations within the Uyeda/Miyamura family.

Several interesting examples come from Hershey Miyamura's wartime experiences. After extraordinary valiant and brave service, he was forced to suffer through several years as a prisoner of war in Korea. Family photographs provided him with a valuable source of information while he was imprisoned. Michiko showed us a letter he wrote from that prison camp specifically thanking her for the photographs. Hershey's return to the United States in 1953 also provided a catalyst for the exchange of pictures. After Hershey's Korean experiences, he was awarded the Congressional Medal of Honor (see Figure 85).[1] Chiko recalled:

> *I guess after Hershey came back and being that we were always clipping whether in a newspaper or [from something else], somebody [always] had a picture. So, they'd give us one, and before you know it, we'd make copies and everyone had one. And, . . . by then, . . . my Dad was into taking pictures. . . . And, so then, he'll make a bunch of them, and that's where it started as far as the family . . . having all pictures.*

The Uyedas also shared in these events. Grace Uyeda showed us album pictures celebrating Hershey's homecoming—one of many albums made by the Gallup newspaper photographers and given to family members (see Figures 86 and 87). All members of the Uyeda/Miyamura family share a pride in his achievement and national honor which is symbolically represented in their photographs of Hershey. These images also serve as a recognition of the honor brought to the Miyamuras and to the family name, an especially important value to Japanese and Japanese Americans.

A brisk exchange of pictorial information through personal photographs has been taking place among the seven Miyamura siblings since the mid 1940s. Often the person who shoots a particular photograph or

Figure 85. Official 8 x 10 U.S. government photograph of Hershey Miyamura being congratulated by President Eisenhower in October 1953. After serving in the all Japanese American 442nd, Hershey was sent to Korea. He was awarded the Congressional Medal of Honor for heroic acts and spent three years as a POW in Korea. Courtesy of the Chiko Miyamura Herrera Family.

Figures 86 and 87. Two photographs made by a Gallup newspaper photographer who gave copies to Grace Uyeda, Terry Miyamura, and other family members. These photographs were kept in an album made by Grace Tomoko Uyeda, showing ceremonial parts of Hershey's elaborate hero's welcome back to his home town, Gallup, New Mexico. Hershey and his father, Yaichi Miyamura, are seated directly behind the speaker in the bottom photograph; Hershey's wife, Terry Tsuchimori Miyamura, is seen holding a bouquet of flowers as Hershey receives congratulations in the top photograph. Courtesy of the Grace Tomoko Uyeda Family.

pays for its processing and printing will make six copies to send to all the brothers and sisters. The Miyamura sisters seem to be central in the exchange of pictorial information. Although the men sometimes participate in the interaction between the families, communication seems to be usually from Nisei women to Nisei women. In her extensive study of Japanese American kinship ties, anthropologist Sylvia Yanagisako found that Nisei sisters take on a central role in communicating with siblings and relatives: "Sisters . . . are the kin keepers who facilitate communication, coordinate gift exchanges, and bring kin together" (1985: 217). In short, Nisei women, especially sisters and sisters-in-law, maintain and, indeed, can transform the network of family relationships:

> *Nisei sisters are in much more frequent contact than brothers. Many sisters see or telephone each other two or three times a week. Some are in daily contact with at least one other sister and a woman with three sisters in the area may speak to all three in one day. Sisters do not hesitate to telephone each other on the spur of the moment or to drop in on each other without advance notice. During my interviews, Nisei women frequently called their sisters and mothers to check on the accuracy of some piece of information such as a marriage date. Spontaneous acts such as these provided evidence of women's accessibility to their sisters and mothers, and their willingness to phone or visit each other for no other reason than to "keep in contact" (1985: 215).*

We found that in the Uyeda/Miyamura family, part of keeping in contact included the sisters sending photographs to one another as an important part of their communication among themselves. It became clear the sisters absorbed this responsibility in conjunction with gift exchanges and organizing family parties, reunions, and other types of family gatherings.[2]

In these ways, personal photographs find a culturally logical place within the lives of a people who are intensely concerned with the value of exchanging family information and maintaining family ties. This use of personal photographs is a reflection of how Japanese American kinship relationships, in general, are maintained. In the Miyamura family, as in Yanagisako's case studies, this includes the exchange of mortuary offerings known as *koden* which are exchanged within the extended family, including all Uyeda and Miyamura kin (1985: 22, 227, 234–35). Yanagisako says: *Koden* "is another medium through which sibling sets affirm their continuing presence as a family in the Japanese American community" (1985: 227). She also specifies other forms of communication carried out by the sisters:

> *Nisei wives uniformly arrange and make preparations for family gatherings that bring relatives together, take charge of sending wedding, birthday and graduation presents (to friends as well as relatives), handle most of the correspondence with geographically distant relatives, and (without exception) send Christmas cards (1985: 92).*

In other words, Nisei women generally consider social activities as well as domestic activities part of their family work. In retrospect, and in the context of this study, it is only natural that the exchange of family photographs be added to this list of social activities, responsibilities, and, perhaps, obligations.

We found many other examples of sharing photographs across these two families. Frank's second wife, Grace Uyeda, and her daughter, June, have apparently shared photographs taken and developed by Frank with the Miyamura sisters. Chiko related the following set of examples:

> *I grabbed as many as I could and Michiko grabbed quite a few of them too, and then I think she wanted copies of the ones we had. I guess June didn't care one way or the other and so Tomoko-san had this box of loose pictures. . . . I asked her if she had any of myself. I said, "I remember a picture, Frank had a picture in one of his albums . . . I had black bloomers on and . . . one leg of the bloomer was down under my knee and the other one was up above my knee. . . . Whatever became of the picture?" So, Tomoko-san said, "I don't know but if you'd like to look through." Because she had a box of loose pictures. . . . So, we looked through there, but I did not find that one.*

Family members may want to have as complete a collection of family images as possible, and this, in turn, may have required an active sense of competition.

Chiko Miyamura Herrera's Photograph Collection

As a result of their exchange of photographs, all of Yaichi Miyamura's Nisei children, particularly the daughters, have extensive collections of photographs (see Figure 88). One of the better examples is Chiko Miyamura Herrera's collection. It has provided us with many illustrations of how a large number of photographs can be organized, displayed, and stored. Chiko's collection includes at least eleven albums, many "bunches" (rubber-band-bound bundles) of photographs kept in boxes, as well as envelopes of color photographs, studio photographs mounted in cardboard mats, and framed photographs displayed on household walls and pieces of furniture. For instance, we discovered that Chiko had organized her photographs into the following categories: (1) her family of origin, that is, the Miyamura family before the children grew up and married; (2) Chiko's siblings' families, especially Chiko's nieces and nephews; (3) Chiko's own family—her husband John Herrera and their children; and (4) her grandchildren. These photographs were gathered into bundles that were either stored in envelopes or bound with a rubber band or some other tie. Like the Nagano materials from the Los Angeles area, we were presented with a very large collection of photographs.

Chiko used many walls and many areas of her house to display photographs of her extended family (see Figure 89). In her entrance hall, for instance, we found photographs of her son, Michael (b. 1944), and his nuclear family (see Figure 90); and in an adjacent space, we saw individual portraits of her grandchildren, Michael Herrera, Jr., (b. 1970) and Charis Herrera (b. 1967). In the living room, she has photographs of her daughter, Nancy Herrera Ortiz (b. 1940) and members of her nuclear family on the same wall. Photographs of her parents, her other children, and grandchildren appear in framed photographs on furniture in the living room and bedrooms.

Figure 88. Color portrait of Miyamura siblings standing behind Chiko taken during their 1982 family reunion in California. Left to right: Shigeko (Shig) Miyamura Sasaki, Kei Miyamura, Momoko Miyamura Saruwatari, Michiko Miyamura Yoshida, Hershey Miyamura, and Shizuko (Suzi) Miyamura Tanikawa. Courtesy of the Chiko Miyamura Herrera Family.

We found an interesting pattern of presentation on the walls of the hallway that lead to the bedrooms (see Figure 91). Here, she displayed the high school graduation photographs of her nieces and nephews —a representation of achievement that is also very familiar to Anglo American households. The graduation portraits were sent to her by her nieces and nephews, so the photographs are organized generally by the year they were sent. The value on learning, as illustrated in the successful completion of schoolwork, is promoted by these images; this display seems perfectly logical to cultures that value achievements in education.

The Miyamura Japanese side of the family is represented on one wall and the Herrera Spanish American side of her family is displayed on another. This "together but separate" grouping is similar to the way most Nisei think of the "Japanese" side of their family as opposed to the Herrera Spanish American or "American" side. Chiko's arrangement is basically a way for her to sort kinship relationships while simultaneously keeping her family intact as a unit. This pictorial representation conforms to a pattern of lateral breadth rather than consanguineal depth, as noted by Yanagisako (1985: 223).[3] This model of display produces metaphors both for tradition and change, and for patterns of integration, acculturation, and, as Yanagisako suggests, transformations.

By far the largest portions of Chiko's collection were found either carefully arranged in photograph albums or bundled neatly in boxes. The latter were neatly organized in groups, such as "Suzi's bunch," "Momoko's bunch," "Michiko's bunch." Chiko has planned to put them into albums as something to do during her retirement.

Chiko's Photograph Albums

Chiko's albums are devoted to the weddings of each of her siblings, their children, and several nieces and nephews, all of whom she is very proud. To simplify our discussion, we will focus on just two of Chiko's albums—albums that seemed quite complete and ones that offered evidence of Chiko's intentional organization of information and communication.

Examples of groupings of photographs as displayed on the walls of Chiko Miyamura Herrera's house. Courtesy of the Chiko Miyamura Herrera Family. Original Polaroid photographs by Lynne Horiuchi.

Figure 89. In the living room, daughter Nancy Herrera Ortiz's family.

Figure 90. In the entranceway in Chiko's home, son Michael and Martha Kettle Herrera's family.

Figure 91. In the hallway to bedrooms photographs show the juxtaposition of "Japanese side" on the left and the "Spanish side" on the right.

The first one, dubbed "the White Album" by project staff because of its white covers, is best classified as a family album. It focuses on Chiko's family of origin, namely, her parents, Tori and Yaichi, and her siblings. Unlike George Nagano's album which is dedicated to his wife, it is less concerned with the family she helped to create—her family of procreation which included John Herrera, her husband, and their five children. This material is found in a separate volume.

The White Album is also significant because we found considerable space allocated to her cousins—specifically members of the Uyeda family. Chiko's organization brings together the Miyamura and Uyeda families in the same album; there are pages dedicated specifically to Frank Uyeda and his nuclear family. This helped us understand how Chiko was classifying "family" and how close the two families were to one another.

The White Album contained a total of sixty-six black-and-white images mounted on twenty-two pages, as well as thirty-six loose photographs. Although much of the album is made up of snapshot photographs and is much less complex than George Nagano's album, Chiko also integrated a variety of photographic forms into her album. For instance, in addition to snapshots, we found: a copy of one of Yaichi's early passport photographs, a copy of Frank Uyeda's photograph made for his naturalization papers, several studio portrait photographs, Yaichi's cropped copies of these studio portraits, official U.S. government photographs of Hershey Miyamura's Medal of Honor award ceremony, one newspaper photograph, and postcard photographs. Since Chiko had not personally used a camera with any regularity over the years, many of her photographs were gifts from other people and sources. A substantial number were taken and developed by either Frank or Yaichi.

This album does not follow a chronological organization; instead it consists of sections devoted to different subjects. For instance, we found sequences of pages that focused on such topics as Chiko's mother, the Emperor's Birthday, Japanese American picnics, Chiko's father, Chiko's cousins (especially Kika, Frank, and Grace Uyeda), her father's seventy-seventh birthday, her sisters (especially Michiko, Susie, Shigeko), and her brother Hershey's Medal of Honor ceremony.

Unlike George Nagano's materials, very few pictures in this album were captioned or labeled; occasionally we found a date or signature associated with an image. In other words, the explicit presentation of important contextual information was missing. Fortunately we could interview Chiko about the album's organization and use. Chiko stated that her purpose was to put together an album of her "Mother and Dad and Holiday pictures." Beginning with an honorific tribute to her mother, we found three photographs of Tori on the first page: one of her mother's funeral bier (see Figure 92), a studio portrait of her mother holding Chiko as a baby, taken in Japan (see Figure 22),[4] and an individual portrait of Tori. When asked why she had started her album this way, Chiko answered: "Well, I don't know . . . maybe because when she did die, when she did pass away, really, I felt real bad. That was a *bad time* for me . . . and I guess that's why I stuck it in there in the beginning." Chiko discussed the emotional importance of the funeral bier photograph. She felt a sense of pride in the recognition that was paid to her mother by friends and family: "It is important. You see all

Figure 92. Tori Miyamura's funeral bier (Gallup, N.M., 1936) as it appeared in both Chiko's White Album and her Dog Album. A very similar photograph was included in George Nagano's album, "Nagano's Mother 1910–1952." Courtesy of the Chiko Miyamura Herrera Family.

the flowers that she received? . . . There was flowers all the way down the sides too—that they couldn't get them in there [in the picture]." Chiko's response suggests a therapeutic function to album-making. It provides a marked contrast to many Anglo American albums, which are made to celebrate only the happy, good times in life, not the sad or hard times. Although Chiko's reasons for putting these funeral pictures in her album are related to her emotional ties to her mother, the inclusion of these photographs reveals a traditional attention given to the end of life (see Figure 93). We are reminded of how George Nagano also featured a remembrance of "Mother" throughout his extensive album.

Another characteristic of Chiko's White Album is the attention she gives to "reunions."[5] Reunion photographs appear repeatedly in several

Figure 93. Flowers placed at the grave of Chiko's mother, Tori Miyamura, as seen in a snapshot taken by Yaichi Miyamura on Memorial Day 1959—just one of several Memorial Day observations documented in both Uyeda/Miyamura and Nagano albums. Chiko's sister, Michiko Miyamura, said, "When you have been away for a long time, the first thing, if you have parents, you go and place flowers on them [their gravestones] to say, 'I am home.'" Courtesy of the Chiko Miyamura Herrera Family.

of Chiko's albums. There are also photographs of celebrations that have brought the family together: nieces' and nephews' weddings, Yaichi Miyamura's seventy-seventh birthday, the Japanese American National Museum's dinner celebrating Hershey as their guest of honor. For each of the numerous reunions and celebrations, there are also photographs of the entire extended family and pictures of the Miyamura siblings. These types of photographs were distributed to members of the Miyamura family when they traveled and visited with each other to lend support for all kinds of activities. We learned more about how these pictures were shared; copies were found in the collections of the other Miyamura siblings. Once again, we see the family reunited numerous times. Here we have the symbolic version of "reunion"—this time between the covers of a photograph album.

The second of Chiko's albums examined for this project has two Scotch terriers on the front cover, surrounded by autographs of family members and friends (see Figure 94). As might be expected, it came to be known as the "Dog Album" by the project staff. This album contains sixty-seven black-and-white photographs mounted on thirty-seven pages, as well as forty-seven loose images. Images are not arranged chronologically but rather according to groups of people, such as siblings, employees, and friends, among others. The content of this album is foreshadowed by the signatures of fifteen people that appear on the album's front cover. The image of the dogs is insignificant.

This album differs from the White Album in most of its photographic content. However we were surprised to see that Chiko began both albums in exactly the same way. The same pictures of her mother's funeral bier and the picture of Tori holding Chiko appeared as loose photographs between the first two pages of the album. When asked why she did this, Chiko explained that she placed them there to preserve them and so she wouldn't lose them.

After these introductory photographs, however, this album is constructed around a different kind of social organization than we found in the White Album. The majority of this album focuses on Chiko's siblings, family relatives, and friends, as well as employees and regular patrons of the family restaurant businesses—people who became close

Figure 94. Cover of Chiko Miyamura Herrera's Dog Album.

friends. For instance, we found pictures of Chiko's sisters, Michiko, Shigeko, and brother Hershey. We also found photographs of Frank Uyeda's wife Grace, also addressed as Tomoko-san by family members.

This album includes many people classified by Chiko simply as "friends"—acquaintances from either her school days or the work place. Here the album begins to reflect the complex social organization of the area. The diverse multiethnic composition of Gallup is seen in part as Chiko included pictures of her Mexican, Italian, Spanish, Native American, and Anglo friends. Chiko's comments on this album helped us understand the importance of these pictures:

> *those [pictures] I've got some from high school. They didn't come out very clear. But, then it's just one of those little Brownies. And, I'd take pictures . . . just to be taking pictures of kids from high school. And,*

*they wanted to see what it looked like when it came out. And, then, a
lot of them were so fuzzy. They said, "Oh, I don't like that picture" . . .
I said, "It's all right. I'll keep it." . . . I kept them even though they're a
little fuzzy, but, at least I know who they are . . . the time they took it
and all that. And, they were friends. That's why I keep them, whether
they're good or not.*

For Chiko—and probably for most family photographers—the memories of these relationships were much more important than aesthetic characteristics or stylistic features of the photograph.

Chiko continued her album by including pictures of women who worked as waitresses in her parent's restaurants, and sometimes we even identified spouses or siblings of these employees (see Figure 95). Examples included pictures of Arsislo, (a waitress's brother); Helen (a waitress who worked for Yaichi Miyamura); Frank and Helen; Senni and Russel; among others (see Figures 96–98). This particular configuration of social relations, focusing on friends from the workplace, was also found in the Nagano materials. I suspect that the inclusion of these people is closely related to what George Nagano was doing when he included photographs of himself at his different jobs along with the pictures of his fellow workers.

Work, in this sense, seems an extension of the family unit, when coworkers are treated as members of the extended family. Chiko's album also contained photographs of waitresses taking the Miyamura children on picnics to the Petrified Forest and points along Route 66.

For the most part, pictures in this album are stripped down to the representation of people; in fact, every mounted picture includes at least one person, and all but two of the loose pictures feature people. Their location in physical space or other contextual features of their appearance seems less important than their existence in the pictures. Chiko seemed primarily interested in the importance of her relationships with individuals and groups of people more than celebrating specific events, dates, activities, accomplishments, and the like. Chiko seemed to be paying homage to important people in her life. The album represents a network of interpersonal relationships—ties that are socially and personally significant to Chiko and her family. In a symbolic sense, Chiko

Figure 95. A page from Chiko Miyamura Herrera's Dog Album including snapshot portraits of her work-related friends. On the left, we see Arsislo Savedra, the brother of Stella Savedra, a waitress at the Lucky Lunch, Yaichi Miyamura's restaurant in Gallup, N.M.; on the right, we see Helen Des Murtas, a family friend. In the middle photograph, we see George Redbird, a Navajo and regular patron of the Lucky Lunch. Courtesy of the Chiko Miyamura Herrera Family.

Figure 96. Additional pages of Chiko's Dog Album were devoted to her sisters, her personal friends including Lucky Lunch waitresses, and her school friends. As described by Chiko, in the left photograph we see Chiko and Mary Shibata on Railroad Avenue, the old Route 66; in the middle, we see Ethel Pino, a Navajo friend, in the back of Cotton House, the house of one of Gallup's well-known pioneers; and on the right, Margaret Catgenova, Madeleine Negra, and Ruth Ann Symington, Chiko's school friends. The diversity of Gallup's ethnic composition is documented in this collection of personal photographs. Courtesy of the Chiko Miyamura Herrera Family.

Figure 97. Another page from Chiko's Dog Album showing Mary Des Murtas and Edith Tartar, two of her school friends and co-workers at the Lucky Lunch restaurant. Courtesy of the Chiko Miyamura Herrera Family.

Figure 98. Snapshot captioned "Frank and Helen." Helen Des Murtas worked as a waitress at Yaichi Miyamura's Lucky Lunch restaurant until she married Frank, a Cherokee Indian; later they moved to Oklahoma. Courtesy of the Chiko Miyamura Herrera Family.

Figure 99. Chiko also included this graduation photograph of her school friend, Nettie Ruth Harter. Caption reads: "With Love, Nettie '37" as found in Chiko's Dog Album. Courtesy of the Chiko Miyamura Herrera Family.

is maintaining the existence of this network by keeping people close together in album form.

The Dog Album's view of a real life network of personal relationships has resulted from people's strong desires to share their lives with one another by exchanging personal photographs. This album contains explicit evidence of this type of sharing in the form of inscriptions—comments written either on the face or the back of the photograph. For instance, some inscriptions read as follows: "To my Dearest Chiyoko-san," "With Love, Arsislo to Chiko," "With Love. Nettie '37" (see Figure 99). On the back of one loose photograph, we read: "This was taken June, late 1943. It's a funny one. If I take a better one I will send you one. Anderson, Calif[ornia]. Kimiko Fujiyoka." And on the back of a picture of a woman named Alice, we read: "I guess you have seen Alice's picture that I gave her. It's the same picture but I got it made special in this size because I wanted to give you one. Sincerely, Asatio Kowayashi." These examples contain the same meta-communicative features found in George Nagano's album. In Chiko's albums, it becomes clear that there was considerable conscious effort given to sending and even exchanging photographs with relatives and friends. This album also provides evidence that photographic gifts were given to acknowledge and indeed maintain important interpersonal relationships.[6]

Frank Uyeda's Photograph Album

The photograph album made by Frank Kozo Uyeda contains 405 black-and-white photographs mounted on seventy-two pages. The earliest pictures date to 1916, the year he returned to Gallup after six years of education in Japan. This album is untitled and undedicated. However, inside the front cover we read the following hand-written directive: "Turn the leaves of the album And enjoy it again" (see Figure 100). In retrospect, it appears that Frank was writing this statement to himself since so much of the album's contents are about his own personal existence. There is little indication that the album was produced for his natal nuclear family. We found less family emphasis than we discovered in albums made by George Nagano or Chiko Miyamura Herrera. However, we feel comfortable calling it a "family album" because Frank did

Turn the leaves of the album
And enjoy it again.

Figure 100. Inscription written by Frank Kozo Uyeda on the inside cover of his seventy-two-page photograph album. In a similar way, George Nagano also decided to include a brief directive comment at the beginning of "Nagano's Mother 1910–1952" (see Figure 29). Courtesy of the Grace Tomoko Uyeda Family.

include pictures of his wife, Grace Tomoko Yamasaki, their children, Glen and June Uyeda, his sister, Kika Uyeda Taira and her family, as well as his in-laws, such as members of the Yoshiga family (see Kinship chart in Appendix B) (see Figures 101–3).

This album covers the years 1916 to 1933. We have not been able to learn when Frank actually began organizing the album or the motives he had for making it. Unlike George Nagano, Frank left very little in the form of written materials, as either diaries, captions, or notes in the album. Deriving the organization and structure of this album has provided us with much more of a challenge; family members have not been able to confirm that the unnumbered album pages are in the same order that Frank originally intended them to be. It is clear however that a total of thirty-five photographs have been removed from different album pages. Grace Uyeda told us that family members had borrowed individual photographs to have them copied for their own collections, but the originals were seldom returned.

Another feature of this album involves the origin of its images. We

Figure 101. An enlarged snapshot made by Frank Uyeda during a picnic near Gallup attended by members of both Uyeda and Miyamura families. This grouping includes Frank's mother, Tazu Uyeda (second from left, his sister, Kika Uyeda Taira (third from left), and his aunt, Tori Matsukawa Miyamura (on far right). Courtesy of the Grace Tomoko Uyeda Family.

Figure 102. As part of Frank's "family album" we found that he included snapshot of his sister, Kika Matsushita Uyeda Taira, and her family. Here we see Frank's nephews and nieces (Kika and George Taira's children): left to right, Robert, Kei, Mary, and George, Jr., in what may have been an Easter photograph, c. 1936 in Gallup. Courtesy of the Grace Tomoko Uyeda Family.

Figure 103. Two snapshots from page 41 of Frank Uyeda's album. Frank's wife, Grace Tomoko Yamasaki Uyeda, appears of the left of both photographs. In the right picture, Grace is standing next to Mrs. Yoshiga. Courtesy of the Grace Tomoko Uyeda Family.

believe from several accounts that approximately 80 percent of the photographs were taken by Frank; and many of these were processed, mounted, and sometimes cropped by Frank himself. We are certain that this album is very much a product of Frank's vision and, in turn, his personal statement of life.

From interviews with members of the Uyeda/Miyamura families, we have been able to reconstruct and review some of Frank's life between 1919 and 1933. For instance, during these years, we learned about his enrollment in Heaton Elementary School and Gallup High School. And by 1933, Frank had married for the second time, and had fathered his second child. For the most part, however, the album depicts pieces of Frank's life before marriage, and relates to his relationships with the Uyeda/Miyamura families before the onset of his own family responsibilities. With these general parameters in mind, we can examine certain topics that Frank selected to show about his life in photographic form.

One of the most prominent topics in Frank's album is his education (see Figure 104). This emphasis differentiates it from most Anglo

Figure 104. Portrait snapshot of Frank Uyeda as a schoolboy in a "yukata" or cotton kimono standing in front of his school in Japan, c. 1915, just before he returned to Gallup, New Mexico, to enter the Heaton School. Courtesy of the Grace Tomoko Uyeda Family.

American examples—albums that might include only a few graduation pictures from successive levels of school. However, Frank's album includes much more. Three major and two minor sections of the album are devoted to his educational experiences.

First, attention is given to his relationship with the Heaton Elementary School—the school where he rapidly learned English. Frank photographed his one-room schoolhouse at Heaton (see Figure 105) as well as his teacher, Mrs. Brooks (see Figure 106), several of his classmates, and the interior of his classroom. Frank also included a photograph from the Gallup Elementary School. These album pages are followed by photographs that illustrate a second educational setting—his life at Gallup High School. Special and lengthy attention is given to Frank's classmates and especially to his participation on the Gallup High School football team. Frank played on this team between 1920 and 1924. We also see Frank in photographs with his best friend, Richard Fujii; Richard also attended Heaton School and Gallup High School and, later, went to Purdue University with Frank.

Figure 105. We find additional attention to learning, virtually never found in Anglo American family albums, in Frank Uyeda's snapshot of the interior of his one classroom school. Frank attended the Heaton School to improve his English immediately after returning to Gallup from his other schooling in Japan. Courtesy of the Grace Tomoko Uyeda Family.

Figure 106. As part of Frank's attention to education, we find photographs taken in several school settings such as this 1920 snapshot of Frank Uyeda, close friend Richard Fujii, and Mrs. Brooks, Frank's teacher at the Heaton Elementary School, located just outside of Gallup. Courtesy of the Grace Tomoko Uyeda Family.

Figure 107. Formal portrait of college-bound graduates from 1924 Gallup High School. Frank appears second from the left in the top row (his surname is misspelled—Ueda—in the caption), and Frank's close friend from Gallup, Richard Fujii, is seen third from the right, top row. Courtesy of the Grace Tomoko Uyeda Family.

The third focus on education is found in Frank's photographs taken at Purdue University in Indiana during 1924–25 (see Figure 107). Frank's year at Purdue is documented with numerous pictures of campus buildings (see Figure 108) and football games. We find a picture of Frank seated at his desk in his "dormitory room"—he actually boarded in a private home off campus (see Figure 109). Here he is seen surrounded by his books, furniture, tennis racquets, school pennant, and even a framed photograph hanging on the wall. In this section of the album, Frank also decided to include several photographs of his Filipino and Anglo classmates (see Figures 110, 111) as well as members of the family with whom he boarded. Perhaps these photographs resulted from an activity described by Monica Sone in *Nisei Daughter* as follows:

During the last few weeks on campus, my friends and I became sentimental and took pictures of each other at favorite sites. The war had

Figure 108. During Frank's year in Indiana (1924–25), he took many photographs on the Purdue campus, including the grounds, various buildings, athletic fields, and campus activities. These snapshots appear in many sections of his album. Courtesy of the Grace Tomoko Uyeda Family.

Figure 109. In addition to exterior shots, Frank took the time to document his living and studying environment at Purdue—an area he personalized with careful attention. Photographs like this are generally not found in Anglo American albums from the same time period or contemporary times. This image is similar to "at work" photographs we found in other Japanese American albums. Courtesy of the Grace Tomoko Uyeda Family.

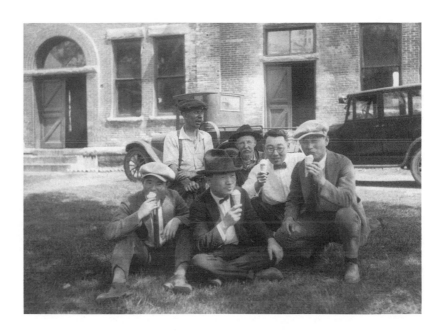

Figure 110. Six of Frank's Purdue colleagues enjoying ice cream cones in front of a campus building in 1924. Asians and particularly Filipinos are heavily represented in Frank's classmate photographs. Groupings like this frequently appear throughout Frank's album, but the names of individuals were seldom written down. Courtesy of the Grace Tomoko Uyeda Family.

jolted us into a crisis whose impact was too enormous for us to fully comprehend, and we needed these small remembrances of happier times to take with us as we went our separate ways to various government camps throughout California (1953: 62).

The large number of total photographs devoted to Purdue is interesting in light of the fact that he spent only his freshman year at college. According to Grace Uyeda, Frank dropped out when he learned that even if he completed the four-year engineering program at Purdue, he would not be eligible for an engineering position because he was not an American citizen. It is tempting to claim that this disproportionate number of pictures devoted to the Purdue experience was compensation for his decision not to complete his program of studies. Regardless of this interpretation, it certainly illustrates the positive values placed on higher education by Frank, and by Japanese Americans in general.

Figure 111. Two snapshots from page 51 of
Frank Uyeda's album showing Frank's college
friends, taken both inside and outside of Purdue
facilities in January 1925. Courtesy of the Grace
Tomoko Uyeda Family.

Figure 112. Class portrait showing students in the Japanese language school near the Japanese Free Methodist Church. This school was housed in an unused railroad car in Gallup, New Mexico, and was rented for one dollar a year from the Santa Fe Railroad. Courtesy of the Grace Tomoko Uyeda Family.

Two additional school settings are found in pictures from the 1930s. Frank included group portraits from the Japanese language school (or *Nippon Gakuen*) that was formed by the Gallup Japanese Americans to make sure their children learned Japanese. The school was held in an old railroad box car that had been converted into a classroom (see Figures 112 and 113). This car was situated next to another box car that housed the Free Methodist Church.

We found interesting regional differences here. Japanese-language schools existed in virtually every Japanese American community throughout California by the 1930s. These schools were operated by a church or Japanese association, and were often taught by church ministers, their wives, or well-educated persons in the community (Waugh, Yamato, and Okamura 1988: 169). There are numerous reports that the Japanese-language schools were not popular with Japanese American

Figure 113. Frank Uyeda's portrait of members of the Japanese Free Methodist Church and Sunday School in Gallup, New Mexico, c. 1942. From 1939 to 1955 a railroad car donated by the Santa Fe Railroad Company was used by the Japanese American community for activities. Courtesy of the Kay Taira Family.

youth. Consider these findings from a study by anthropologist Christie Kiefer:

> *Most of my nisei respondents [in San Francisco] had gone to Japanese school for at least a few years. For the most part, they remembered it as an unpleasant experience and not very educational experience. It took them away from leisure activities enjoyed by their non-Japanese peers, and the atmosphere of the Japanese school was usually stiff and stuffy to their way of thinking. They were taught proper etiquette, such as bowing and polite forms of speech; respect for authority, especially of parents and teachers; personal qualities of thrift, honesty, diligence, punctuality, neatness; and some Japanese government and history. Many students, especially the boys, seem to have spent the better part of their class time plotting escape (1974: 21).*

Other situations, including Gallup, were described by Grace Uyeda as follows: "Most of the [Gallup] children went to American schools. . . . My children were too small [for Japanese school]. But, when I was in Hawaii, I went to Japanese school and American school. We all went. Japanese school started at 7:00 in the morning and ended at 8:00, and we went to American school from 8:30 to 2:30. But, here, they just went to American school. And, later, Mr. Shinto . . . started Japanese school. . . . They didn't go too long before the war broke out. . . . They never had it any more. So a lot of these children [who] grew up here can't speak any Japanese. And, then, if you don't practice you forget." The Japanese-language school in Gallup lasted only four years.

Regardless of the Nisei's ambivalent feelings toward this school experience, photographs were taken of "student times" by the adult generation and saved in albums. In this case, Frank, as a Japanese American, was signifying a reverence for his Japanese past, a determined effort to remember it, and to celebrate the continuation of learning as a key value among Japanese Americans. In Frank's album, these images are juxtaposed with photographs of Glen Uyeda's (Frank's son by his first marriage) class in the Gallup Elementary School (see Figures 105 and 114). In short, we found Frank making many references to some facet of educational experience—much more than is generally found in comparable Anglo American albums. The pictorial manifestation of value placed on education is clear.

While the themes of "becoming educated," "attending school," and "attaining educational degrees" are easily stated as central concerns, it is also clear that Frank was celebrating his relationships with Japanese, Japanese American, and American cultures. He was acknowledging connections to cultures, institutions, as well as groups of people by including this combination of pictures in the same album.

A second topic featured in this album recognizes Frank's affinity for games, sports activities, and related forms of competition (see Figure 115). Baseball, football, and car racing were his favorites. We found several photographs of Frank as a member of a baseball team while he was a student in Japan before returning to Gallup. Later, in the 1923 edition of *Zillho Zhuni*, Gallup High School's yearbook, we

Figure 114. Two snapshots from page 58 of
Frank Uyeda's album. He extended his attention to education by including pictures of
his children's school experiences. Frank took
photographs of the kindergarten classes of his
children, Glen and June Uyeda, at the Gallup
Elementary School, c. 1935. Courtesy of the
Grace Tomoko Uyeda Family.

Figure 115. Snapshot of Frank (in sweater-jacket) taken in Japan while he played on the Kyushu baseball team, c. 1915. Courtesy of the Grace Tomoko Uyeda Family.

read the following inscription next to a portrait of Frank Uyeda:

Name—Frank Uyeda—Nickname "Ada." Pet expression, "Touch Down." Description, Total breadth, 1 yd. Fat, weighs 2 or 3 hundred. Straight, well groomed and tidy. Favorite Hangout, Pool Hall. Worst habit, late for school. Favorite Pastime, playing pool. Editorial Comment:—Good football man with all his faults.

We have already noticed that in photographs, from both Gallup High School and Purdue University, significant attention was focused on athletics. From Frank's high school days, we found many photographs of individual football players specially cut from other pictures and rearranged on an album page according to Frank's own design (see Figure 116). We also found many scenes of Frank and his teammates in "action" shots, taken from either practice sessions or actual game conditions (see Figures 117 and 118). Again, Frank edited many of these pictures by cutting out irrelevant action and content, and he constructed his own layouts of sports pictures on individual album pages. To this avid interest in football, we add Frank's photograph of an informal boxing bout (see Figure 119) as well as his involvement in baseball and car racing. Frank included many photographs of his teams, his teammates (either posed as a group or as individual portraits for personal identification) (see Figure 120) and even his coaches. These images are very similar to team photographs that were previously identified in George Nagano's album. These examples provide a quick comparison of ethnic variability within both regions. The composition of Gallup's football team illustrates the multiethnic composition of the Gallup area; the Nagano pictures from Los Angeles are considerably more homogeneous Japanese American.

These sports photographs provide good examples of how attention to a real-life activity can be transformed into a parallel emphasis in the symbolic version of that activity, namely the photograph album. This connection can also be applied to the attention Frank gave to his education, to sports, to competition in general, and to his affinity for automobiles and car racing.

Figure 116. Page 13 of Frank Uyeda's album, one of several pages in which he carefully composed portraits of members of the 1922 Gallup High School football team. The ethnic diversity of Gallup is again apparent in the composition of this sports team. Frank appears in the top row, second from the left. Names of his teammates include John Lang, Moses Lopez, Alex Kitchen, Ralph Yoder, Lon Alexander, Ray Pickard, Tom Moore, Spencer Bellman, Jack Hamilton, and Coach Fernandez. Courtesy of the Grace Tomoko Uyeda Family.

Figures 117 and 118. Two examples of the Gallup High School football team in action, c. 1924. Frank added a sense of dramatic action to these photographs by shooting them from ground level. He edited these shots by cutting them, along with most of his other football pictures, for customized placement in his album. Courtesy of the Grace Tomoko Uyeda Family.

Figure 119. Frank's snapshot of a boxing match taken on the grounds of the Heaton School, c. 1920, as found in Frank Uyeda's album. George Nagano placed a similar snapshot in "Nagano's Mother 1910–1952," showing two men in a sumo wrestling match at a Japanese American picnic at a beach in Venice, California. Courtesy of the Grace Tomoko Uyeda Family.

Figure 120. A portrait of the Kyushu baseball team as found in Frank Uyeda's album. Frank played on this team around 1915 when he attended school in Japan before returning to the U.S. and his family in Gallup. Courtesy of the Grace Tomoko Uyeda Family.

Figure 121. Two snapshots found on page 14 of Frank Uyeda's album; this page, captioned, "My Ford—Before & After," acknowledges Frank's intense interest in cars and his talent for automobile mechanics. He was frequently given a car by his parents. Courtesy of the Grace Tomoko Uyeda Family.

The third focus of Frank's photographic documentation—automobiles and car racing—contains many pictures of people and cars; some appeared on carefully organized pages that seem dedicated to Frank's interest in cars. The album page entitled "My Ford—Before and After" is one of the better illustrations of this interest (see Figure 121). Here we found five photographs taken in 1921 of the Ford car he received from his mother, Tazu. Frank's love for cars was mentioned several times in interviews with Grace Uyeda:

> *Yeah, his folks used to give him everything he wants. . . . [And] his father (Heizo) used to buy him every year a new car, since he was the only boy and he was the last boy. They wanted a boy so bad that he was the last one in the family. Above him were four girls. . . . [H]e always wanted car, car. He used to buy car all the time.*

Figure 122. An older Frank Uyeda seated on the front fender of his car as seen in a snapshot placed on page 61 of his album. Courtesy of the Grace Tomoko Uyeda Family.

Some of the special attention and preferential treatment given to Frank is understandably connected to gender politics in Japanese and Issei culture. First-born sons were accorded deferential treatment, special privileges, and authority by other members of the household.[7]

This collection of images demonstrates an unusually strong involvement with cars. Snapshots of a family member or friend standing in front of the family car, or sitting on the car's front fender are much more common (see Figure 122). A quick comparison with George Nagano's photographs of people juxtaposed with cars, in more conventional poses, makes this point quite well.

Frank's interests in engineering and automobiles contributed to his emergence and recognition as a talented car mechanic. He made sure

Figure 123. Snapshot of Frank's father, Heizo Iwase Uyeda, standing with a fellow worker at the entrance to the coal mines near Gallup, c. 1921. Courtesy of the Grace Tomoko Uyeda Family.

he had photographs of the garages where he developed his skills in car racing. Frank's interest in cars extended to competition. Several images and complete pages of the album included carefully cut photographs documenting scenes of car racing. Relationships between cars and people were themes that stretched throughout the entire album.

Another theme that connects the photographs taken by Frank Uyeda and Yaichi Miyamura to George Nagano's album is attention to the workplace. We noted in Chapter Three that studies of Anglo American albums seem to avoid deliberately any mention of or reference to work or labor. But in Frank's album, we found several pictorial references to working and employment. For instance, on early pages we noticed photographs of people standing in front of entrances to the shafts of coal mines (see Figure 123). These mines were very important to the early immigrant life of the Uyeda family. Tazu and Heizo owned a series of four boardinghouses that catered specifically to the miners. We learned that Frank's father, Heizo, worked in the mines, and, in fact, Frank worked there during his summer vacations from high school.

Frank's album also contains pictorial reference to several garages and his work as a car mechanic (see Figure 124). We have already mentioned that the album contains a large number of automobile photographs —family cars, racing cars, people seated in cars, standing in front of cars, among others. After his year at Purdue, and possibly utilizing his interest in engineering, Frank developed considerable skill as an auto mechanic. We learned from his wife, Grace, that after 1925, Frank worked in as many as seven different garages, which included Gurley Motors, Navajo Chevrolet, Hushman Motors, Central Motors, Henry Yoshiga's Garage. In addition, he had his own garage—Frank's Auto Service—from just after the war until 1968.

In this chapter we have emphasized both the structured content and the structured use of family album imagery. As a form of interpersonal communication, the exchange of photographs can serve as a form of symbolic bonding to bring together members of the family who are living away from each other. The placement of the photographs also functions symbolically, whether on a household wall or in an album. It

Figure 124. A snapshot of one of several garages and service stations where Frank Uyeda either worked or spent lots of time, exercising his skills as an auto mechanic and furthering his car racing ambitions. Courtesy of the Grace Tomoko Uyeda Family.

remains for us to offer a more extensive discussion on how photograph albums can be understood as a pictorial medium for statements of belonging and the communication of unity. We now turn our attention to the symbolic representation of unity and belonging—important themes shared by both collections of photographs in this study.

Chapter Five

Exploring Identity in Japanese American Photograph Albums

We examined how George Nagano combined his photographs with a variety of other informational sources to construct a very personal and complex album—a portrait of his life with his wife, Seki. We also studied the Uyeda/Miyamura practice of giving away and exchanging personal photographs. We cited the social significance of habitually sharing pictorial information among members of extended families. These observations of what people do with their photographs can now be taken several steps further by asking what these habits do to and do for people in these networks of distribution and exchange. Values attached to themes of family and cultural unity have been cited as keys to explaining why people make personal photographs and why they organize their collections in certain ways. But how are these values and these photographic expressions related to concepts of both identity and ethnicity? Is it possible to see how ordinary people express their feelings about changes in the lives of family members and family generations through time? What can be said about the ways people show they have not changed—that they maintain similar feelings, values, beliefs, customs through several generations? Are family albums better at showing how people remain consistent or change their ideas about who they are and how they should live? What happens to these questions when asked of immigrant ethnic groups of people who have undergone dramatic relocations and changes in their lives? Here is where the consideration of personal photography as a way that family members feed back information about themselves to themselves becomes very important. This should be seen as a dynamic continuous process of people taking pictures, looking at pictures, organizing pictures, taking more pictures, and so on—a process based on personal and cultural needs for expression, learning, and communication.

Feedback Functions of Photography

Throughout our study of Japanese American photographs, we have implicitly asked why people feel their personal pictures are so important, and, secondly, why people are attracted to photographic imagery in general. One answer was provided by anthropologist John Adair when he reviewed our research materials. He suggested that "the deeper significance of photography in social, cultural, and biological contexts lies in how photography serves as a means of promoting human cybernetics." Here Adair was reminding us of the roles played by feedback in all forms of human existence—Adair's colleagues, John Collier, Jr. and Malcolm Collier, state the case as follows:

> *All forms of self-expression are varieties of feedback. Our very intelligence depends on a constant renewal of awareness, and it is through feedback in painting, balladry, storytelling, and in modern man story reading and film viewing, that we acquire and retain our intelligence about ourselves and our life experiences (1986: 118).*

Adair added a direct reference to our Japanese American materials: "These pictures feed back to the individual, family, and community what is essential for establishing your identity and lifeline. I think photography can be viewed in that context."

The significance of feedback is accentuated when we treat all forms of photography as communication and examine carefully the content of feedback messages. Not everything gets "told" or photographed for album content. Again, we are working with a symbolic process in which selective patterns of information are repeated, retold, and revitalized in visual forms. All photographers, even ordinary people making snapshots, are selective in their picture-taking; the content of personal photographs is anything but the result of random thoughtless behavior.

Album photographs continue to "return information" in positive contexts—they continue to remind people of who they've been, who they are, and how they want to be remembered. There is always a sense that these pictures have been made to be looked at by personally important people.

Personal photography encourages us to establish identities as individuals, but individuals who inevitably have relationships to social groupings, personal affiliations, and cultural memberships. One example comes from a field experiment. Anthropologist Edmund Carpenter introduced cameras and photographs to several groups in New Guinea. As part of that fieldwork, he stated:

> *A photographic portrait, when new and privately possessed, promotes identity, individualism: it offers opportunities for self-recognition, self-study. It provides the extra sensation of objectivizing the self. It makes the self more real, more dramatic. For the subject, it's no longer enough to be: now HE KNOWS HE IS. He is conscious of himself (1975: 458).*

Adair added to this perspective when summarizing the significance of the Japanese American project: "I look at projects like this as a way of giving the individual, family, and community a sense of self-respect —of perpetuating family and community tradition, through the use of visual means, specifically through the use of cameras. . . . And it seems to me it draws the community together—it gives the community a sense of identity through visual means."

Historically, we know that people have used oral and written traditions for reasons of cultural feedback. People have remembered and recounted stories, legends, myths, and tales about their beliefs, origins, changes, and contemporary status to keep track of themselves and to pass on information from generation to generation. With the advent of mass-produced cameras and processing facilities, ordinary people were offered new media, new opportunities, to develop a new form of *pictorial tradition* (see Chapter Six). People could include visual descriptions and details that were previously limited to verbal expressions. This relatively new means of "reporting life" was enhanced by pictorial ways of defining human identity and existence. But how do people take advantage of these pictorial opportunities, and how do these opportunities let people communicate these kinds of information?

We now turn to an exploration of how the Japanese Americans in our study expressed senses of identity, belonging, and ethnicity through the construction and use of their photograph collections. How does the personal use of cameras and the content of personal photographs function as symbolic expressions of social relations, frame of reference, belongingness, and unity?

Expressions of Ethnic Identity in Photograph Albums

We introduced questions of ethnic identity in Chapter One. Expressing an identity includes conscious and unconscious statements that somehow define the matrix of personal and social relationships that people share with other people, places, objects, activities, and events. That is, people express who they feel they are, in large part, by how they form parts of larger wholes, and, in turn, how they differentiate themselves from 'others.' In addition to connections to natural and physical environments, people's relationships to supernatural and metaphysical environments are also important matters:

> *like any other form of social identity, ethnic identity is essentially sub-jective, a sense of belonging and ultimate loyalty. . . . Given man's capacities for cultural elaboration, he . . . can, on the basis of* group definitions of belonging, *develop complex formal systems of identity and group social stratification (De Vos and Romanucci 1975: 3, 5; emphasis in original).*

This emphasis on social relationships is very much in line with comments made by authoritative sources on Japanese society and culture. Several social scientists have suggested that attention to social relations and social interaction is fundamental to understanding Japanese society. Ways and means of tying people together into identifiable groups are more important than stressing how people are independent autonomous entities. For instance, Chie Nakane stresses attention to social groupings as follows:

> *In any society, individuals are gathered into social groups or social strata on the basis of attributes and frame. . . . The ready tendency of the Japanese [is] to stress situational position in a particular frame, rather than universal attribute (1970: 2).*

Nakane is using the word *frame* as in *frame of reference;* frame expresses a particular way people are united to one another and way they "belong" to social groups and institutions. Nakane adds: "*Frame* may be a locality, an institution or a particular relationship which binds a set of individuals into one group" (1970: 1). The establishment and recognition of this model of ethnic identity is composed of a particular configuration of relationships with people, places, activities, events. There is general agreement that the Japanese identify themselves by their positions in social frames rather than by individual attributes (Nakane 1970). Christie Kiefer provides us with a nice summary statement of this perspective:

> *Japanese life is group life; the changes experienced by a person throughout his life are also experienced by the groups of which he is a member. Those groups share intimately the credit for his achievements and the responsibility for his difficulties, and he shares the credit and responsibility for theirs. These influences extend outward, both in space and in time, from his biological presence (1974: 185).*

Part of group identity refers back to an observation made earlier—that the basic building block of Japanese group identity and Japanese social structure is rooted in the notion of *ie* or household:

> *The essence of this firmly rooted, latent group consciousness in Japanese society is expressed in the traditional and ubiquitous concept of* ie, *the household, a concept which penetrates every nook and cranny*

of Japanese society. . . . The ie *comprises household members . . .*
who thus make up the units of a distinguishable social group. In other
words, the ie *is a social group, constructed on the basis of an estab-*
lished frame of reference and often of management organization. What
is important here is that the human relationships within this house-
hold group are thought of as more important than all other human
relationships (Nakane 1970: 4–5).

But what can be said about family photographs in relation to these
formulations of social frame and identity? Is it possible to see how
Japanese Americans have transformed *ie* through their family album
photographs? Family photography offers many opportunities to express personal and socially accepted demonstrations of identity. People
symbolically offer clues to their own identity by appearing in pictures
juxtaposed with other humans and with nonhuman objects. There is
agreement that people voluntarily and enthusiastically appear in personal photographs that document and reveal positive aspects of their
lives. In most cases, people do not appear in pictures (1) when they do
not want to, (2) with people they intensely dislike, (3) with people with
whom they do not want to be affiliated, (4) in distasteful or unpleasant situations. Sociologist Lynn Blinn suggests that frequency counts of
certain types of pictures and picture content in photograph albums may
provide quantitative measures of identity. She feels that the "greater the
commitment to an identity, the more pictures there will be that represent and reinforce that image" (1985: 21). In this perspective, people
will have themselves photographed in preferred associations. People
will select and save greater numbers of images that document their preferred relationships with people, places, activities, and events than ones
with which they wish to have little or no association.[1]

The relevance of intended associations and juxtapositions should be
extended into the future, to include the ways people wish to be remembered. These images represent preferred ways of making an appearance
in photographic form, and, in turn, preferred ways of being "seen" and
remembered by anticipated viewers.

Clearly, then, a family album is a significant vehicle of identification. People take photographs and organize them in specific ways to make such statements as: "This is who we have been, and this is who we are." Their albums are private advertisements for themselves. But how does the pictorial content of these Japanese American albums inform us about their ethnicity? What symbolic uses of these pictures further our understanding? Examining the Japanese American albums along this line of inquiry gives us great insight into identity—specifically in how we see people highlighting social relations by juxtaposing themselves with other people, with certain places, things, and events. It logically follows that album content can be examined as a map or index of personal relationships, to preferred patterns of belonging.[2] It is to this theme of "belongingness" that we now turn.

Belongingness in Japanese American Culture

The theme of belongingness seems very well suited to two focal points of our study, namely ethnic identity and an analysis of photograph collections. For instance, in a general overview of the meaning of ethnicity, anthropologist George De Vos examines the significance and influence of such factors as racial uniqueness, economic bases, religion, aesthetic cultural patterns, and language. He concludes:

> *In brief, the ethnic identity of a group of people consists of their subjective symbolic or emblematic use of any aspect of culture, in order to differentiate themselves from other groups. These emblems can be imposed from outside or embraced from within. Ethnic features such as language or clothing or food can be considered emblems,* for they show others who one is and to what group one belongs. . . . *As a subjective* sense of belonging, *ethnicity cannot be defined by behavioral criteria alone. Ethnicity is determined by what a person feels about himself, not by how he is observed to behave. Defining oneself in social terms is one basic answer to* the human need to belong *and to survive (1975: 16–17; emphasis added).*

This theme of belongingness may be all the more important with immigrant groups of people who have experienced or are undergoing dramatic changes in geographic location or regional affiliation, as well as changes in personal, social, and cultural circumstances.

Scholars have given considerable attention to the value Japanese and Japanese Americans place on belongingness, group cohesion, and unity. For instance, Chie Nakane states that in Japanese society,

> *A man is classified primarily according to the group to which he belongs (or the individual to whom he is attached); assessment is in terms of his current activities, rather than the background of his birth (1970: 104).*

Lebra reinforces this view of identification when she discusses a guideline of Japanese childhood:

> *The Japanese child is thus encouraged to develop a strong sense of belongingness and total commitment to the group to which he happens to belong, and is inculcated with the motivation for status identification and role performance (1976: 150).*

Our speculation is that much of this psychological and cultural orientation has survived in Japanese American culture, especially among Issei and Nisei generations. Studies by Befu (1965), Berrien, Arkoff, and Iwahara (1967), Conner (1977), Kiefer (1974), and Levine and Rhodes (1981) have attempted to determine the dynamic relationship of Japanese and American value systems in succeeding generations of Japanese Americans. For instance, some argue for considerable retention even into Sansei (third generation, children of Nisei), while others stress almost complete acculturation into Anglo American culture. There is ample evidence that for Issei and Nisei, Japanese values associated with family solidarity, such as reciprocity, obligation to parents, and interdependence remained strong (Kikumura 1981: 135).

In turn, we sought to understand better how the Japanese Americans in our study used their cameras and photograph collections to satisfy

Figure 125. Portrait of Michiko Izima, George Nagano's "private Japanese school teacher" in Victoria, British Columbia, Canada, in 1913–14. This type of photograph reflects a respect that Japanese and Japanese Americans had for their teachers. This image is very similar to ones that Frank Uyeda put in his album showing Mrs. Brooks, his teacher at the Heaton School near Gallup, New Mexico (see Figure 106). Courtesy of the George Nagano Family.

the important impulse "to belong," "to fit in," "to be connected" to others in meaningful ways. Specifically, we discovered that the Japanese Americans in our study identified themselves through a pattern of their relationships with family members, educational institutions and classmates, athletic groups (formal and informal), church groups, and work partners. But how are these examples of belonging visualized? How is this emphasis on group affiliation represented pictorially in family photographs? Is there a difference in the nature of belonging when talking about groups of people with whom one lives compared to groups of people one meets outside the home? Is the sense of belonging as a child significantly different from belonging as an adult? Do Japanese and Japanese Americans share a sense of belonging to school groups and, most important, to families in similar ways? If so, are similarities or differences evident in family albums?

One important context of belonging found in the albums of George Nagano and Frank Uyeda stressed relationships to learning and the process of education. Both George and Frank paid ample tribute to their schools and their teachers (see Figures 125 and 126). A clear statement about the value of school was made by Michiko Miyamura Yoshida, one of Chiko's sisters:

> *And this is why my son went to school, because number one, education is the most important thing to a Japanese family. Education is the one factor—that is the first and most important thing when you raise your children is they've got to have an education. This is planted in them when they're very young . . . when the time they start school.*

Chiko Miyamura added the following comment in another interview:

> *I think Japanese people as a whole have always had that competitiveness among them. So that each family does try . . . and I'm sure my Dad [said] you kids got to make certain grades and you can't let the next guy get ahead of you, and that was in every family. They wanted the children to get ahead as far as school [was concerned] which nearly all the Japanese here in Gallup have tried to excel in their grades.*

Figure 126. This formal school portrait is captioned "Gallup Nippon Gakuen (1928—April), New Mexico." *Gakuen* means language school, here organized for Japanese American children. Chiko's sister, Momoko Miyamura, is seated fourth from the right in the front row. And Chiko's father, Heizo Iwase Uyeda, is second from the left, top row. Courtesy of the Chiko Miyamura Herrera Family.

School-related references were consistently found in other photograph collections examined as part of the Japanese American Family Album Project, e.g. albums belonging to Toy Kenegai and Rownea Ichihara as well as the Maruyama and Kambnara families.

Similar attention to student life and school membership was highlighted in a family album entitled "Okamoto Family Crest" made by a Japanese American family living on the East Coast.[3] In one case I found a snapshot, taken during the camp years, that showed eleven female students and teacher posed outside a building. The caption reads: "Yone Watanabe (Okamoto), first row left, with her Sunday School class at Heart Mountain Relocation Center in Wyoming." Another example from the camps comes from the Nakai family interned at Poston, Arizona;[4] this image shows eighteen students seated around a table during a tailoring class, and later in the album there are shots from a tailoring class picnic. In the Okamoto album I found a picture that was nearly identical to the image of Frank Uyeda sitting at his desk at Purdue University. The caption reads: "Allen Okamoto studying in his dorm of Lehigh University." But others in this album conform to the preference of being shown in the company of his colleagues. One photograph shows Allen sitting with a classmate on the steps of a university building ("Allen attending Lehigh University in 1940 after two years at the University of Pennsylvania"), and in another we see Allen with two classmates dressed in their graduation robes ("Allen Okamoto graduated from Lehigh in 1942 with a degree in chemical engineering").

Issues of cultural continuity become relevant again when we learn that attention to school group membership remains an important part of contemporary Japanese photographic habits. Lynn Blinn found that the Japanese families in her study liked to have pictures of their children in school-related contexts. In one case, a professional photographer was hired to make a photograph to accompany an application for a prestigious preschool. She also found pictures taken on the first day of school, and, she learned that, unlike American experiences, professional "photographers accompany students on school field trips, outings and field days. They tend to exclusively shoot group pictures" (1986: 17). These pictures are made available for purchase by students and parents, and they are published in their school yearbooks.

School-related photographs offer us examples of belonging to certain kinds of groups that are not classified as residential units. These groups are referred to as *dantai* in the literature on Japanese and Japanese American culture. We gain additional information on the significance of lateral or horizontal kinds of personal and social relationships. Nakane reminds us that "the criterion by which Japanese classify individuals socially tends to be that of particular institution, rather than of universal attribute" (1970: 3). In this context, the designations of "professor" or "student" are attributes, "whereas 'men of Z University' is a frame" (1970: 2). Nakane continues: "Such a group consciousness and orientation fosters the strength of an institution, and the institutional unit (such as school or company) is in fact the basis of Japanese social organization . . ." (1970: 3). Thus, our attention is drawn to associations with educational institutions and to similarities between Japanese and Japanese American culture. In album photographs made by Japanese Americans, we are given evidence of the importance of belonging to certain schools and groups of classmates, on primary, secondary, and college levels. The existence of cultural continuity seems clear in this case.

A second sense of identity and relationship involves another example of *dantai,* namely church membership. Sociologist Harry Kitano offers several observations that justify attention to this sense of belonging and to previous ideas on family:

> *Where the new immigrant was without family, the church served in a family role, supplying the feeling of group participation that the family had provided in Japan. . . . Christian churches had much to offer the new immigrant in the way of employment and Americanization. . . . Churches often provided mission schools, preschools, and kindergartens (1976: 59).*[5]

The literature acknowledges the significance of membership in certain church groups and participation in a regular round of church-related activities (see Figure 127). Modell has noted that both Buddhism and Christianity were considered legitimate in the Los Angeles Japanese community, and affiliates shifted from one to the other. He added: "Japanese religious organizations in Los Angeles were typically "American" in the voluntary, competitive, and somewhat ad hoc quality. . . . Both Christian and Buddhist organizations took on social-welfare functions, the former more than the latter. Both participated in the usual variety of American church-community activities—baseball leagues, Boy Scouts, and the like. . . . Both religions displayed a tendency toward federation, Christianity again more than Buddhism" (1977: 76–77).[6] Belonging to a specific church is another way people create and maintain personal and cultural identities. Kiefer notes:

> *Most nisei think the churches exert a stabilizing and integrating influence in the ethnic community as a whole and on young people in particular. For the church-going nisei, the church is the community*

Figure 127. An 8 x 10 enlargement of a formal Japanese American wedding portrait taken at the Bethlehem Mission on San Pedro Street, Los Angeles, in February 1917. A fascinating set of comparisons between people on two "sides of the isle" with mostly Japanese Americans on the right and Anglo Americans on the left. Anglos played important roles in the development of Protestantism among the Los Angeles Japanese, first through missionary activities and later in advisory capacities (see Modell 1977: 76). Courtesy of the George Nagano Family.

counterpart of the family—it exposes the young to a value scheme which is broadly cooperative and tolerant, avoids extremes, and emphasizes social responsibility rather than individual choice (1974: 38).

In this context, church membership has not gone unnoticed in the photograph collections in our study. We saw how much attention George Nagano gave to both his and Seki's ties to church groups. These included Buddhist and Christian organizations, specifically Methodist and Baptist denominations. Japanese Americans adopted a flexible approach to religion brought to America by the Issei; they might participate in social functions of both religions, but they would attend to the religious aspects of only Buddhism (Kitano 1969: 85–86). George's album illustrates the shifting of affiliations from Buddhist to Christian affiliation mentioned by several authors (see Modell 1977).[7] Although the groups were distinct, Los Angeles Japanese Americans participated in the social events of both. We saw in Chapter Three that George included in his album cut-out newspaper advertisements for the Koyosan Buddhist Church Obon festivities and snapshots of the Obon dancers (see Figures 62 and 63) as well as many references to Christian churches. Kitano reported that Japanese parents of either Buddhist or Christian religions usually agreed that "it doesn't matter what church you go to, as long as you go to church" (1969: 87). To belong seems to be the important factor.

A third domain in our search for pictorial identity involves one's relationships to groups that are officially identified as "teams" of various sorts. For instance, Kitano mentions the ambitious all-Japanese athletic leagues which tended to concentrate on basketball, complete with a national Oriental champion, playoffs, all-star teams, rooting sections, trophies, and so on. Kitano makes the specific points that these teams offered "the usual advantages of participation in a group activity—team and group identification, travel, competition, and rewards" (1976: 60), and that the "Nisei learned far more from these teams than the skills of athletic competition. It was an experience of independence, travel, social interaction, and role-playing. . . . The basketball teams . . . became primary reference groups for many, and a Nisei would often introduce himself by saying 'I'm from the Cardinals,' which meant that he was from Los Angeles" (1976: 61).[8] Some of these forms of membership come from previously mentioned contexts. For instance, both school and church groups sponsored athletic activities and teams. We have documented many examples from both the Nagano and Uyeda/Miyamura families where team membership was featured in snapshot photography. Officially recognized teams were better organized in Los Angeles than in Gallup, especially for Nisei—and such teams are still active. This provides us with another example of when regional difference becomes apparent. We noticed how much attention George gave to his involvement in baseball, both as a player and later as a coach (see Figures 128–32). Frank offered a parallel pattern of attention to participation on his Japanese school baseball team, to playing football on the Gallup High School teams, and to football activities at Purdue University.

Figure 128. This snapshot of "family as team" is not unlike the popular Japanese and Japanese American sense of "team as family." Left to right, sons Tyrus, Jack, and Paul Nagano stand in front of their father, George Nagano, on the sidewalk of their "4th Street home" (the Mayfair Hotel) in April 1927. Courtesy of the George Nagano Family.

Figure 129. "Nagano's Ball Team, July 1928." The neighborhood baseball team that George Nagano coached while he lived and worked at the Mayfair Hotel in Los Angeles between May 1924 and August 1930. Courtesy of the George Nagano Family.

Figure 130. Another sport, another lineup. Again, in 1932, George Nagano fields a football team including his sons Tyrus, Jack, and Paul. This snapshot was taken on Omar Street, Little Tokyo, Los Angeles. The caption reads: "4th St. Gang . . . 1932." Courtesy of the George Nagano Family.

Figure 131. Stories told by several family members have included George Nagano's intense interest in playing baseball. His first baseball team is seen in this portrait made in 1912 in Victoria, British Columbia, Canada. George stands fourth from the right, top row. Courtesy of the George Nagano Family.

Figure 132. A portrait of two baseball teams who played against each other when Mr. Miyaki, manager of the Meiji team, visited Victoria, British Columbia, Canada, in 1914, as part of the team's West Coast tour. First baseman, George Nagano, is seated in the front row, fourth from the right. The reader will recall baseball team portraits found in Frank Uyeda's album (see Figure 120). Courtesy of the George Nagano Family.

Other examples of continuity become clear. We found connections among Japanese American personal pictures and a similarity between old and contemporary Japanese photography. For instance, Lynn Blinn noticed reference to sports activities in the collections belonging to Japanese businessmen:

> *One popular custom is for the husband to play golf with a group of business associates, then have a group picture taken by the club in-house photographer. Other pictures will be taken of the husband executing a series of golf swings. I was told that these pictures have strong evidentiary value in confirming his position as a businessman and member of an important group and social class (1986: 18).*

In this case we find markers of an identity that relates leisure, sports, competition, and now work, yet the emphasis remains with group membership and group identification.

A fourth area of attention focuses on how people feel related to their fellow workers and to their places of work. Both Lebra and Nakane discuss the significance Japanese place on "company ties" alongside kinship relations, and that part of identity is located in one's work experience. Nakane states: "In group identification, a frame such as 'company' or 'association' is of primary importance; the attribute of the individual is a secondary matter" (1970: 30).

Reference to the notion of family is involved once again. When discussing the significance of work relationships, Nakane feels that ties between employer and employee are "as firm and close as that between husband and wife" (1970: 14). A relevant example of work-related photography in Japanese society comes from Toson Shimazaki's book, *The Family,* when family members were getting ready for a group portrait:

> *"Mother, the photographer is here," Shota called as he came in. "Change your kimono. . . ."*
> *Her husband shouted into the shop. "Kasuke, everybody, come and get into the picture!"*
> *As a momento, a family photo was to be taken in the garden facing*

the back parlor. The head clerk and employees could stand wherever they wanted, Tatsuo placed himself in front of the azalea. According to the family legend, it had been planted by the founder of the business, Chikuo.

"The women should be in front." Tatsuo directed, and the three women took places on chairs.

"Uncle Sankichi, come a little more to the center. You're the guest. . . ." The apprentice clerk Kosaku and Kasuke's son, Ichitaro, were also in the group" (1976: 26–27).

Contemporary emphasis on work-related photography was found in Blinn's sociological study of family albums made by Japanese living in Houston, Texas. Examples included pictures taken working at a desk, on business trips, and relaxing with co-workers:

All of the husbands were successful businessmen and had numerous business-related pictures. . . . One album contained pictures of the family posed in front of ships at the various ports they visited while on vacation because the husband worked for a shipbuilding company. While the husband often appears formal, unemotional and reserved during family picture-taking, he is allowed to appear informal, drunk and friendly with his business associates (1986: 18).

A comparative example of Japanese American behavior was found in Uchida's book *Desert Exile:* "Before we sat down to any of our company dinners, Papa always lined everybody up outside on our front lawn and took several snapshots with a succession of cameras from a Brownie box camera to a German Rolleiflex" (1982: 19).

When I examined the photographs belonging to the Okamoto family living on the East Coast, I found work-related pictures that were thematically related to examples from the Nagano and Uyeda/Miyamura collections. Captions included: "Richard and William Okamoto and a friend in front of their Oriental gift shop at 13th and Walnut in May 1920"; "Several concessions in Willow Grove Park were started by the Okamoto brothers"; under a photograph of nine colleagues around an office table, "Allen Okamoto's place of employment, Atlantic Refining,

Figure 133. This work-related snapshot appeared on a page labeled "1913," the same page that mentions Seki's work as a telephone operator (see Figure 6). George Nagano's caption refers to himself when he writes: "Dad at work. Mr. Nakane's office. Real Estate, back in 1913–1914." Courtesy of the George Nagano Family.

Research and Development, from 1948 to 1960;" and under a snapshot of Mr. Okamoto seated at an office desk using a telephone, we read: "Dad at General Electric Space Center." Thus it appears that this type of photograph is not limited to working-class occupations.

Compared to Anglo American albums, the two Japanese American examples studied for this project give unusual amounts of attention to work situations. For instance, George Nagano's album is full of job-related pictures, taken from times when he worked as a field laborer, in stores, hotels, churches, or in other jobs (see Figure 133). We made similar claims for pictures of work locations taken by Yaichi Miyamura. We also found examples of Lucky Lunch waitresses in Chiko Miyamura's photograph collection as described in Chapter Four.

But, here, as in all cases, cultural context must be kept in mind. Working in any situation was highly valued for Japanese immigrants, and taking a position in a subservient position was definitely seen as a means to an end. De Vos comments on this situation as follows:

> *Characteristically, a person would submit to an apprenticeship, with the goal of acquiring status through competence, just as [in] a traditional Japanese society, one was expected to submit to a long apprenticeship. . . . A traditional Japanese does not feel it socially or personally demeaning to be in a subordinate position while he is learning. His sense of integrity is not destroyed by adversity. Japanese immigrants to the United States imparted to their Nisei children a respect for authority, even the authority of an alien society—they were to become loyal citizens (1975: 35).*

In other words, we are still seeing a composite portrait of qualities that are valued in positive ways—a statement of people "doing things right" and conforming to a pattern of cultural values. In this context, finding the large number and variety of work-related photographs in these Japanese American collections is not surprising at all. Eventually we may discover that family photograph albums from all societies conform to a pattern defined by only positive aspects of life.

We also found pictorial evidence for a pride in membership in ethnic associations, in community or neighborhood associations. Our clearest evidence of this appears in many photographs of community picnics found in virtually all Japanese American albums studied for this project.[9] For instance, George's album included photographs taken during church picnics and holiday picnics and *kenjinkai* or Japanese Prefectural Association picnics (see Figures 134–37). Kitano calls the annual picnic "the most visible rite" for Japanese Americans:

> *Here in microcosm may be seen the workings of the Japanese-American community as a whole and of the Japanese family through several generations. Thousands of families, congregating in larger groups related to the original ken or province of their forefathers, celebrate their Japaneseness, their sense of a heritage different from the white American culture of which they are a part in day-to-day life. . . . The day [chosen for the picnic] does not coincide with any other traditional Japanese festival, and opinion among Issei is divided about its origins. Some hold that there was never such a thing as a community picnic in Japan, while others maintain that they had them all the time (1976: 62–63).*

Figure 134. Another of many picnic scenes in "Nagano's Mother 1910–1952," here showing members of the Nagano family and friends at the "Santa Maria Picnic" in June 1930. Paul Nagano is on the far left and his mother, Seki Nagano, is standing next to him. Courtesy of the George Nagano Family.

Figure 135. George Nagano took this photograph during the "Market Picnic," which was part of the July 4th celebrations in 1938 at the Arroyo Seco Park in Los Angeles. Courtesy of the George Nagano Family.

Figure 136. One example of celebrating an annual prefectural organization or *kenjinkai* event was recorded by George Nagano on August 18, 1968. Caption reads: "Wakayama Ken Picnic at Elysian Park, No. 9 Section." Courtesy of the George Nagano Family.

Figure 137. Another example of a Kenjinkai picnic appears in George Nagano's color snapshot captioned: "Sat[urday] July 27—1974 Ibaragi Ken Picnic at Brookside Park, Pasadena. . . . See Tyrus take care of food." These picnics occurred just once each year. Courtesy of the George Nagano Family.

We found personal photographs that depicted associations with types of national affiliations, but with much less frequency than previously listed categories.

In a chapter entitled "That Feeling of Belonging" of *The Japanese American Story,* Budd Fudei discusses a variety of voluntary associations that were operating between 1900 and 1910 on the West Coast. In addition to prefecture groups, church groups, and sports teams, he cites examples of merchant and trade unions, the Tokyo Club of Los Angeles, community service clubs, and gambling clubs. Fudei mentions that specific occupations had their own associations, for example, medicine and gardening; there were also clubs where Japanese could play *goh* (a Japanese stone piece game) and *shogi* (Japanese chess), and "a post-World War II organization that has gained wide acceptance is the *Hyakunen* (One-Hundred-Year Club). Membership is extended to those desiring to live to age one hundred" (1976: 128).[10] However, we did not find photographs that documented membership in the Japanese Association (*Nihonjinkai*), nor in other of the groups mentioned by Fudei.

Ties among album-making, personal photographs, and themes of family belonging and family unity are not surprising. We would expect that people organizing a collection of pictures, called a "family album" would emphasize kinship relations. This would seem all the more obvious for a group so concerned with a notion of *ie.* But exactly who gets included in these images, and how are kinship relationships represented in pictorial form? Our first comments relate to two characteristics of kinship groupings, namely people who live together as a residential unit, and relatives who are grouped in a pattern of contemporary (or horizontally related) kin relatives.

George Nagano and Chiko Miyamura Herrera made albums that focused on family relatives in both explicit and implicit ways (see Figures 138–41). As Chiko's sister, Michiko, said in one of our interviews: "I think it's important to know you are a part of this family or that family . . . [it is] something [you] should kind of know." In Condon and Kurata's book, entitled *What's Japanese about Japan?,* we read: "One is part of a group, first and forever. First comes the family." (1974: 87).

Figure 138. Nagano family portrait taken during their New Year's Day gathering, 1934, in Los Angeles, California. Caption reads: "Happy New Year. Whole family 3rd Street home." Courtesy of the George Nagano Family.

Figure 139. Miyamura family portrait taken by an itinerant photographer—"so we all got dressed up," said Chiko—in Kika Uyeda Taira's home, c. 1932. Left to right: Kika Uyeda Taira holding George Taira, Jr., Chiko Miyamura, Hershey Miyamura, Tori Matsukawa Miyamura holding Shigeko Miyamura, Yaichi Miyamura holding Kei Miyamura, Momoko Miyamura, and Michiko Miyamura. Courtesy of the Chiko Miyamura Herrera Family.

Figure 140. Three generations of Nagano family members gathered at the home of Jack Nagano for Christmas Day, 1951, as seen in this snapshot taken by Jack and kept in George Nagano's album. From left to right (top row): Seki, George, friends Mrs. and Mr. Mizumoto; (middle row) Louise (Jack's wife), Tyrus, Paul and his wife Florence; (front row) Tommy, Carol, Jimmy, Steve, and Christine. Courtesy of the George Nagano Family.

However, in cross-cultural studies, verbal (either spoken or written) or pictorial expression of these kinship relationships should not be taken for granted. Some societies prohibit certain relatives from being talked about or even looked at directly. A parallel set of norms —both prohibitions and prescriptions—may exist for family photography. For instance, we should acknowledge personal and cultural reasons for why certain family members are included more than others, and which people are not seen at all. In this regard, we found a curious lack of photographs of Junko, who was George and Seki's only daughter. While George's album addresses the sons and honors the mother, it seemingly ignores the daughter.[11]

Pictorial expressions of "belonging to family" were also found in album photographs that focused on different types of family gatherings. Included here are annual social events such as family reunions, calendar holidays, and picnics, as well as specially recognized birthdays and ritualized religious events. These events frequently include family members from different geographical locations; they also include several generations of family members. As such, people gain a feeling of belonging across generations and through time—a type of vertical continuity that will be discussed in the next few pages. The Japanese American family photographers took full advantage of these occasions.

Family gatherings offer ample opportunity for the demonstration of sharing, unity, and belonging; they also provide many chances for producing photographic evidence of participation in these events and adherence to associated values. The Issei and Nisei consider holidays and life-cycle events as occasions for bringing together "relatives"—members of the immediate and extended family. One example is found in Yoshiko Uchida's revealing account, *Desert Exile: The Uprooting of a Japanese American Family,* where we read: "There was a strong sense of family at these three-generation gatherings and to commemorate the occasion we often had a two-family portrait taken" (1982: 19).

Our study demonstrates how family gatherings were used by Nisei siblings to affirm their solidarity. One way to express this feeling of unity is to write about it. For instance, the significance of one Uyeda/

Figure 141. Extended family portrait taken as part of Chiko's sister's (Shigeko Miyamura Sasaki) daughter's (Candace Sasaki) marriage to John Schiavone, c. 1982.

Miyamura family reunion is found in a poem written by the youngest of the Miyamura siblings, Shigeko Miyamura Sasaki, and placed at the beginning of one of Chiko's albums:

> *Family Reunion—June 20, 1982*
> *Dear brothers and sisters—nephews and nieces,*
> *My how the family circle increases*
> *It's been a long time since we've all been together*
> *So let's make this one last to remember forever*
> *We've all had some bad times, but good times outnumber*
> *Thank you for caring in so many ways*
> *Believe me they've helped in those dark, dreary days*
> *As for myself, at this time please let me say,*

I pray every night in my own special way
"Thank you Lord, for letting me be
From a family of people who are special to me"
God gave me six children with His own special touch
And they've all made me proud—I love them so much.
I'm rich and I'm happy for the treasures are YOU,
And I've always had them—

        "MAY GOD BLESS YOU TOO."

Other ways of illustrating these feelings include taking photographs. In one of our interviews, Michiko said: "I don't enjoy it [taking pictures] . . . I'm not good at taking pictures, but the family's usually always taking pictures, forever, whenever we get together."

Participation in the family event as well as in the picture-making event itself signifies symbolic unity, solidarity, togetherness. Personal photographs taken during these times become a second ordering of symbolic rendition, solidifying ties as they are put into albums or incorporated into the collections of other family members. We have seen this in the example where Frank Uyeda took a picture of his family group at a Fourth of July picnic in 1963. Chiko Miyamura Herrera then included a copy in her family album.

Celebrations, ritual events, life turning points, including religious or personal holidays as well as significant calendar and national holidays, provide points in time and space for the acknowledgment and demonstration of family unity. The Japanese American families mentioned several holidays familiar to Anglo-American society, including Christmas, Easter, Thanksgiving, and the Fourth of July. Birthdays, reunions, graduations, and weddings were also represented in their photo albums. Needless to say, the recognition of these times is not limited to Japanese Americans. All cultures, however, do not celebrate important life events in identical ways. In addition, experiences such as immigration produces changes in personal, social, and cultural circumstances, that, in turn, promote transformations in methods and means of celebration. However, we did discover specific links to Japanese culture when Japa-

Figure 142. A Frank Uyeda photograph (c. 1928) of his Japanese American relatives dressed in traditional Japanese clothing as part of celebrating the Emperor's Birthday, or *Tensho Setsu* (April 30), as found in Chiko Miyamura Herrera's White Album. Chiko is seen third from the left. Courtesy of the Chiko Miyamura Herrera Family.

nese rituals were integrated into American celebrations. One example was mentioned in Chapter Three, namely pictures that showed the celebration of the Buddhist All Souls' Day, or *O-bon* as found in George Nagano's album. According to Smith, "Bon is by far most elaborate of the four seasonal rites directed to the collectivity of the ancestors" (1974: 99).[12] Bon is usually claimed to be an imported Buddhist ceremony that has come to obscure almost completely the old Shinto spirit festival of midsummer; the Bon festival is still one of the most important festivals in Japanese American communities (see DeFrancis 1973: 45). Other examples include celebrations of the Emperor's Birthday found in the Uyeda/Miyamura collections (see Figure 142).[13]

The Japanese sense of belonging was celebrated by both families in our study during special gatherings such as the celebrations of Yaichi

Figure 143. An enlarged color snapshot from an album made and kept by Steve Nagano, one of George Nagano's grandsons. George (on left) is seated next to Reverend Paul Nagano, George's youngest son and Steve's father. The occasion is George Nagano's eighty-eighth birthday—a specially recognized birthday in both Japanese and Japanese American cultures. Courtesy of the Steve Nagano Family.

Figure 144. The cake was designed specifically for George Nagano's eighty-eighth birthday. Perhaps most relevant to this study is the inclusion of the camera shown in the upper right corner of the cake's decoration. "Pop" refers to George's coaching activities, which, in turn, are related to the tennis racquet in the upper right as well as the baseball bat and cap, and sneakers. We also see such Japanese symbols as a turtle for longevity, a pine tree for strength, bamboo for flexibility, and cherry blossoms for felicity. Courtesy of Steve Nagano.

Figure 145. George Nagano, seated next to his grandson, Steve Nagano, being congratulated by Yosh Inadomi, a close family friend, during George's eighty-eighth birthday party. Courtesy of Steve Nagano.

Miyamura's seventy-seventh birthday and George Nagano's eighty-eighth birthday (see Figures 143–45). These are birthdays traditionally observed and celebrated in Japan as auspicious markers of the life-cycle. The eighty-eighth birthday in Japan is called "beiju" and is based on a visual pun playing off the written characters for rice or "beiju" and for eighty-eight or "hachi-ju-hachi" (Robert Smith, personal communication).

Both families seem to have adapted the ritual forms that are normally used in Japan for these birthdays in different ways. In the photographs of George's eighty-eighth birthday, George is wearing a red cap and vest. The color is symbolic of childhood and also expresses joy, felicity, and auspiciousness. However, in Japan, the attire is worn for the sixtieth birthday, not the eighty-eighth. The photographs of Yaichi's seventy-seventh birthday in June 1965 are not dissimilar to an American family group example (see Figure 146); there is nothing in this photograph that distinguishes it as a special celebration as a Japanese way of denoting an important moment in Yaichi's life. In Chiko's album,

Figure 146. A portrait made on June 3, 1965, during Yaichi Miyamura's seventy-seventh birthday—another significant birthday in Japanese culture. Members of Yaichi's nuclear and extended families traveled to Los Angeles to acknowledge this achievement. Chiko said, "We all wanted to be there for this special birthday party." Courtesy of the Chiko Miyamura Herrera Family.

her annotation is simple, with minimal acknowledgment of the special significance of the birthday: "1965 June Dad's Birthday 77 years."

Celebrating these special birthdays provides time for a gathering of the extended family, and for reinforcing family ties through participation in a social activity (see Figure 147). In these two cases, the occasion was accompanied by camera use. Home-mode photography was done to reinforce family relationships; the subsequent selection of these photographs for inclusion in several family albums will afford family members another kind of celebration. A symbolic gathering has been produced—symbolic representation of it will be placed in the family album, to be seen and remembered again and again.

Belonging by Memory: Vertical Continuity

In addition to horizontal relationships, some album photographs stress the significance of vertical continuity—another important topic in the

Figure 147. Portrait of the Miyamura extended family taken as part of Yaichi Miyamura's seventy-seventh birthday on June 3, 1965. From left to right, top row: Kei, Yaichi, Hershey; seated: Michiko, Momoko, Chiko, Suzi, Shigeko. Courtesy of the Chiko Miyamura Herrera Family.

literature on Japanese culture. In Lebra's analysis of Japanese behavior, the notion of belonging is not restricted to a person's contemporary existence or to the confines of one's actual lifetime. In concert with the notion of *ie,* past intimate relationships are also highly valued:

> *It is also common to refer to a frame one previously belonged to, such as one's birthplace, the house in which one was reared, the school from which one was graduated. Belonging by memory thus cannot be overlooked. Japanese identify themselves by both* shozoku *("current belonging") and* shusshin *("origin") (Lebra 1976: 22–23).*

Conceptually, all family albums would seem to be ideal vehicles for two important tasks, namely the communication of unity through time and space, and stating the importance of belonging through memory in visible, pictorial forms. In a sense, we can think of an album (or photograph collection in general) as a storehouse, a holding bin, or even a filing system for views and memories of the past. Indeed, one common reason people give for making snapshots is "the preservation of memories."

As with all other examples of symbolic activity, we can only hold onto bits and pieces of memories. In personal photograph collections, we seem to get clues to positively valued memories much more than negatively valued ones. If this selective retention is stated as a general principle (and a heuristic one at that), details of memorable events and associated picture content must still be considered as situationally and culturally variable. That which is valued in positive ways in one culture may be treated as negative in another.

Our claim has been that personal photographs are selectively taken and organized in albums to help people acknowledge, review, and celebrate the significance of previous social relationships. The Japanese Americans in our study have stressed the need to keep the memories of these relations alive in one way or another. A sense of maintaining ties with the past is very clear in the written statements found at the beginning of albums made by George Nagano, Frank Uyeda, and Chiko Miyamura Herrera. George says: "Boys! . . . This is your family album. Look them over and turn back [the] pages of your childhood day." Frank's statement is simply, "Turn the leaves of the Album and Enjoy it Again."

In Chapter Three we saw how George Nagano constructed and used his album in certain repeated and patterned ways—in what we now understand as ritualized ways—not unlike the ways that memory is maintained by the daily practice of ritual in Japan. George's behavior emphasizes the importance of cross-generational ties. He follows the Japanese custom of treating recently "departed" family members as a continuing part of everyday life, by using photographs to "heighten the effect" of visualizing the departed (Plath 1964: 308–9). In this way, the living can speak directly to the deceased, reporting on a variety of family matters—births, deaths, illnesses, family business, house renovations, graduations, weddings, and the like (Smith 1974). Illustrations of this behavior have been cited in Chapter Three, when George

Nagano informs his deceased wife, Seki, of developments in the family, of their children's activities, of how he remembers their shared moments together. George performed a cultural transformation by using his camera, photographs, and captions in the aid of cultural transmission. Again, we find a way that album photography can function as a vehicle of communication to satisfy and conform to certain culturally accepted values and goals.

When considering the topic of social function, we might ask: What do family photographs do for family members who cannot be in the physical presence of one another? Lebra reminds us that "belonging by memory makes us aware of the symbolic, as well as the social and physical, nature of the frame for belonging" (1976: 23). By focusing on the theme of belonging, we have explored the ways people choose to be linked to each other and to specific groups of people. That is, we are examining how people create and maintain their social organization. In this context, several additional findings receive new significance.

For instance, in both the Nagano and Miyamura/Uyeda families, the Japanese sense of belonging and family has been further reinforced by symbolic journeys which cross generations. Among the photographs of a trip to Japan, we find the Miyamura/Uyeda family celebrating *ohakamairi*. *Ohakamairi* is one ritual for caring for, communicating with, and continuing to revere one's own ancestors. It is performed in Japan at least once during each season of the year. The gravesite is swept, water is poured to purify the site, a prayer is said, and votive candles are lit. At this time, relatives may receive the latest news about family members, be offered a cup of sake, or simply be revered as ancestors. In 1977, Hershey and Terry Miyamura and Alex and Nancy Ortiz went to Japan and visited the Miyamura temple site in Ogawa-machi, Japan, and had the traditional rites performed (see Figures 148 and 149). More recently, in 1983, the same rites were performed by Chiko Miyamura Herrera with her son and daughter-in-law, Gerry and Patty Teshima Herrera, when they went to the Uyeda family graves (see Figure 150).

Once again, personal photography plays an important role. The inclusion of the photographs in the family albums record these as memorable moments of their visit to Japan.[14] The record of these rituals is an example of the continuity of the *ie* and maintaining the memory of the Japanese ancestors in the family in a much adapted form. But, now, understanding of that concept in the Sansei (third generation) is from an American point of view. However, some observers feel that the Sansei, in general, have little understanding of the traditional concept of *ie* and its attendant value system. In the Nisei generation, there is already evidence of a preference for living in nuclear-family households, which they feel are "better" and "more comfortable," given a couple's desire for privacy and independence (Yanagisako 1985: 181).

Steve Nagano, George's grandson, has devoted two of his own albums to his ascent of Mount Manzo Nagano (see Figure 151). This was the first ascent of the mountain; it was undertaken by Steve; his elder brother, Jimmy; their cousin, Dave Nagano (Jack's son); David's brother-in-law, Bob Drescher; and a guide (see Appendix B). They placed a plaque commemorating their ascent on the summit. The plaque incorporates the use of the Japanese Canadian Bicentennial logo and the Nagano family crest or "mon," illustrating the adaptation of a Japanese tradition in a Western context (see Figure 152).

Although the albums are organized in an American format with a sense of humor and adventure, the ascent is symbolic and the plaque is clearly an expression of family honor and pride in one's ancestors. The recognition of Manzo Nagano as an important man in the family is clear. At least for Steve and his Sansei cousins, Manzo Nagano's reincorporation into the family was, in part, due to his recognition as the first Japanese Canadian to settle in Canada. His prestige affirmed both his own and his family's worth since his reputation had an impact on the Nagano family and its shared identity. Anthropologist Sylvia Yanagisako sees this situation for Nisei as follows:

> That the family is a unit of shared identity means not only that its members, through their actions, have an impact on each other's current reputation in the community, but that those actions are evidence of the members' shared past, that is, of qualities transmitted through past generations. . . . Thus, an individual who achieves a prestigious occupation

Figure 148. A photograph made by Alex Ortiz in a Ogawa-machi graveyard in Japan, site of the Miyamura family temple. Hershey Miyamura and his wife, Terry, traveled to Japan to perform the traditional *ohakamairi* ritual in 1977. Courtesy of the Alex Ortiz Family.

Figure 149. Parts of the Ohakamairi ritual include washing the marker, placing flowers, and lighting votive candles at the gravesite. Pictures like this snapshot can be used to show Japanese American relatives in the U.S. that proper rites have been performed—a reversal of pictures of funerals in the U.S. being sent to Japanese relatives. Courtesy of the Chiko Miyamura Herrera Family.

Figure 150. A snapshot of Chiko standing by the Uyeda family ritual gravesite in the fore-ground and the town of Ogawa-machi, Japan, in the background, 1983. Courtesy of the Chiko Miyamura Herrera Family.

Figure 151. Bob Drescher and Jimmy Nagano, one of Manzo Nagano's great-grandsons, place a commemorative plaque on the summit of Mt. Manzo Nagano in June 1979. Steve Nagano designed the plaque and had it custom fabricated for this occasion. Courtesy of Steve Nagano.

MT. MANZO NAGANO

永 野

JULY 25, 1979

PLACED BY: B. DRESCHER, D. NAGANO,
J. NAGANO, S. NAGANO, R.J. SECOR

Figure 152. Photograph from Steve Nagano's
album showing the details of the commemorative plaque he designed and placed on the
summit of Mt. Manzo Nagano. Courtesy of
Steve Nagano.

*or who becomes a community leader simultaneously affirms both his
own and his family's worth. . . . The combined achievements and deeds
of individual members of a family, therefore, create a reputation and
a history for it that extend farther into the past than anyone's knowledge of its ancestors. Present character is interpreted as evidence of
past character. Good conduct is proof of good blood as well as good
upbringing (1985: 237).*

Diary-writing and such modern counterparts as family albums contribute to this sense of sharing and identity. The albums are the symbolic
expression of symbolic acts of family unity. In this sense, the founding
father of the Nagano family is brought together with the fourth generation of Japanese Americans, including a non-Japanese member of the
family who has married into the Nagano family.

In summary, we discovered that two Japanese American families
used their photograph collections to identify themselves with many
levels of social organization, from nuclear and extended families, to
school, work, church, teams, to national affiliations, including both
country of origin and country of new citizenship, and, to a lesser degree,
voluntary associations. In this context, several observations about Japanese culture are relevant: "In theory, the individual does not even exist
as an individual but only as a member of certain larger groupings—
family, school, community, or nation. There are no individuals but only
sons and fathers, students and teachers, citizens and officials, subjects
and rulers" (Reischauer 1965: 150, as cited in Connor 1977: 31–32).
This theory of Japanese culture appeared to us as a reality of Japanese
American culture—but as revised reality. Expressions found in these
photograph collections seem to confirm some connections and continuities between Japanese and Japanese cultures. Again, this is not to say
that the two are identical or interchangeable. It is to claim, however,
that Japanese American traditions and indeed identitites can be seen as
interpretations of Japanese traditions. We have acknowledged several
transformations—whether manifest in the ways a family album was
used to communicate with deceased relatives, the ways photographs
were hung on household walls, details central to celebrating specific

birthdays, behaviors associated with neighborhood picnics, Bon carnivals, or with *Koden* exchanges. All seem to reinforce relationships, the sense of belonging, and membership in groups. We feel safe in generalizing that photographs of group membership found in these Japanese American collections are much greater in number and broader in scope than what is usually found in their Anglo American counterparts.

Chapter Six

Camera Cultures and Pictorial Traditions

In previous chapters, we have demonstrated how individuals have used pictorial images in symbolic ways, to store, communicate, and reinforce their messages. We have also discussed how the exchange of photographs can function symbolically to maintain family unity and communicate changes in the family. We have attempted to examine relationships between personal pictures and general concepts of ethnicity, cultural identity, and social values. In our two case studies we have been continually impressed with the ways that personal, social, and cultural identities find specific representation in family album imagery. Equally outstanding is the way these identities can be referenced, realized, and remembered through a family's use of these photographs.

We have asked how ordinary people create symbolically realized worlds with their cameras and family photographs. But we have also attended to how our taken-for-granted abilities and opportunities to make family photographs fit into our modern world of multiple representational forms. What kinds of generalizations can be made from this kind of study and this project in particular? What are some implications of our findings? Moving from some particulars of Japanese American photography to several types of generalizations and overviews helps us get to larger questions of what this ability to create pictures means in terms of representation, communication, and feedback.

Studies like this beg questions of how culture fits into home-mode communication, in general, and family photography, in particular—and how pictorial communication fits into culture. But what is meant by "culture"? What are the roles or functions of culture in the process of visual communication that we have been studying? How does culture influence ordinary people's use of their cameras and their pictures? And how do these types of cameras and pictures influence culture?

Human Cultures—Camera Cultures—Kodak Cultures

If we insist that people use their cameras and pictures in culturally structured ways, what do we mean? We have studied behaviors that are driven by both culture and technology—what both people and machinery promote and allow. We are constantly dealing with an interaction of what culture-bearing people bring to photography and what pieces of photographic apparatus bring to people and culture. While people use cameras, there is also a sense of cameras using people. It is as if *both* have a say in what happens. In the former we are dealing with traditional notions of culture; but in the latter we are suggesting something less orthodox—namely the notion of camera cultures, and, in this case, the relevance of "Kodak culture."

Susan Sontag makes several references to "camera culture" in her popular book, *On Photography* (1977). And Halla Beloff even titles her book *Camera Culture* (1985). However she never defines what she means by the term, saying "in the domain of photographing, there are rules, and etiquette and courtesies, as there are in any activity" (1985: 34). In several chapters of *Snapshot Versions of Life* (1987) I have suggested the term *Kodak culture* and even added notions of "Polaroid people" and "Sony society" replete with "Beta babies" and "Instamatic infants."[1] For many anthropologists, this use of the term *culture* is unwelcome and possibly accepted only as a playful metaphor.

But if we follow this metaphor, what might it suggest? We must surmise that camera culture has many subcultures, each with its own set of norms for appropriate and inappropriate behavior, manifest and latent functions, implicit and explicit models of learning, and accumulation of knowledge, conventions, ethics, etc. This case is easily made for alternative genres of "photographic practice"—that is, fine art photography, forms of documentary photography (street photography, reconnaissance), photojournalism, types of commercial photography (fashion, advertising), among others.[2] But this list only includes professional practices.

We must add the most practiced and popular forms of photography, namely nonprofessional examples or what is most frequently referred to as "amateur photography." We learn from Seiberling (1986) and Schwartz and Griffin (1987) that even the term *amateur photography* has become ambiguous. For instance, we might be talking about early travel photography undertaken by the independently wealthy or upper-class students as part of the grand tour, or we might be describing the popular participation in nationally recognized or locally directed camera clubs. The making of snapshots and albums as part family photography must now be recognized as just one of several models of amateur practice, and, as I have suggested, a subculture in itself. One conclusion is that camera culture includes many different histories, practices, conventions, and discourses—the description of each can even change through time.

But is this concept of camera culture driven more by mass consumer technology than human participation with this technology? Do people from all over the world participate in camera subcultures in the same way? Do camera models produced for mass consumers carry implicit sets of instructions—ones that prescribe social uses in addition to mechanical ones?[3] Are culturally divergent peoples producing homogeneous versions of life? Or, to come back to our earlier question, does the culture of the camera-users ensure that people from different cultures participate in Kodak subculture in different and distinct ways? This line of inquiry leads us to our second important relationship between culture and photography.

The second way of integrating the significance of culture focuses on what individuals and groups of people bring to, and in a sense, take away from their uses of camera technology and their photographic results. While previously we asked what people do *with* their cameras and pictures, we are now focusing on what cameras and pictures do *for* people. In this sense, we mean that people behave with the cameras and pictures in ways that conform to their cultural dictates. This, in part, is why we investigated the "Japanese past"—for what had been said about both Japanese and Japanese American culture, and for relationships of cultural values to photographic habits. These questions have been at the heart of our study.

Here is where we return to issues of universal versus culturally specific behavior. Do all people from all cultures participate in "Kodak culture" in identical ways? The answers to these questions must be both yes and no. People are quick to generalize that snapshots are the same all over the world, and that the snapshot genre of representation is immediately recognized regardless of national, geographic, or cultural origin. On a superficial level there is some truth to these claims. But studies like the *Japanese American Family Album Project* demonstrate, first, that when we look further, differences do, in fact, exist, and second, that culturally related reasons begin to explain patterns of similarities and differences found in personal photograph collections from different parts of the world.

We have seen that in comparison to Anglo American collections, the Japanese Americans in our study did give unusual amounts of photographic attention to matters of work, school, church, last times, and funerals. For instance, we do not find the Eastman Kodak Company or the Polaroid Corporation publishing advertisements for taking cameras to work, or making snapshots at gravesites or funerals. These are not considered appropriate choices for what Kodak advertisements label as "the times of your life."

Another lesson is that differences may be a part of similarities, or that differences may be more a matter of degree than kind. For instance, birthday parties and related celebrations are commonly included in family photograph collections. But, upon closer inspection, we may discover that certain personal birthdays or nationally recognized holidays get more attention than others. We do not find pictures taken during the Emperor's Birthday in Anglo American albums, nor is the seventy-seventh or eighty-eighth birthday of a family member an important photographic event. We found examples of the former in the Uyeda/Miyamura collections, and examples of the latter in the Nagano collection.

Other comparisons involve the "look" or aesthetics of personal photographs. A slowly emergent collection of home-mode studies from different parts of the world is offering more evidence for a diversity of "glances" and "gazes" rather than absolute uniformity and homogeneity. We found that the more recent snapshots in the Nagano collection looked different from many of the earlier ones. For instance, the earlier images, more associated with the Issei, are more group oriented; the more recent ones, especially ones associated with the Sansei, seem to feature more individual appearances of people than groups. In addition, the earlier photographs we examined seem to have a different sense of composition than contemporary examples. For instance, we found several examples of deep focus landscapes that featured an object in the foreground, usually the tree, and an expanse of countryside in the background. This model of composition emphasizing distance is absent from the more recent images in these photograph collections. Previous framing that attended more to surroundings is replaced by a central attention to people arranged at the center of the snapshot. There is also some indication that this happened more quickly in Gallup than Los Angeles. But many other variables need to be explored before these observations can go beyond the speculative stages of discussion.

In summary, we see two trends when we compare the earlier photographs to later ones in these Issei and Nisei collections. On the one hand, we see changes, but mostly in terms of surface characteristics of image content. The photographs depict changes in fashions of clothing, hair styles, activities in photographs, and, in some cases, changes in expression—especially smiles—and postures. In one obvious example, we see cowboy outfits replace kimonos. But on a deeper level, we find the attention given to the significance of family, work, achievement, group experience, and honor reminiscent of values associated with Japanese culture.

Camera Cultures, Media Socialization, and Identity

Another relevant issue in the integration of cameras and culture surfaces when we consider how camera subcultures might be supplementing a general process of socialization, especially one of family socialization. That is, how do various photographic records contribute to the on-going process of learning and acknowledging cultural belonging and identity?

One implication of our close attention to matters of identity and ethnicity presented in previous chapters is that people want to recall their pasts in special ways—with personalized records of who they have been, where they have come from, and how they have changed. Personal photography affords ordinary people efficient and effective ways of preserving parts of the past in conjunction with a recognition of innovations and new pieces of their lives.[4] But what for? Why this attention, effort, and expense?

One answer is that people fully intend to preserve their albums to show to people in the future. This motive is directly related to human needs for feedback—a theme mentioned in earlier parts of this book. Photograph collections offer family members new methods of accomplishing old tasks—members of one generation can communicate information to successive generations in highly descriptive and informative ways. In turn, members of younger generations can learn about their elders through these customized views of life. Cross-generational and intrafamilial communication, informal means of education, and socialization are all central to this use of photograph collections.[5] Herein lies one way that family members can maintain a sense of cultural continuity—of keeping ethnic identity alive and creating new transformed versions of identity—while they simultaneously monitor and participate in an on-going process of acculturation.

Continuity and change necessarily involve the process of "media socialization." Usually this term is used in reference to mass media—that is, how people learn about the ways of their own society (and sometimes other societies) through their exposure to feature films, television programs, newspapers, magazines, novels, and even comic books. In cross-cultural contexts, the term *media acculturation* may be more appropriate. Anthropologist Christie Kiefer suggests the role of media in this general process as follows:

> *In a multicultural milieu the processes of acculturation and development are intertwined. . . . For instance, during the early stages of the ethnic minority group member's life, the important people for him are likely to be his parents, siblings, and playmates. His position on any hypothetical cultural continuum is likely to be strongly affected by the positions of these people on the same continuum. Later, as his social horizons broaden, he is influenced by the mass media, his teachers, schoolmates, ministers, even by lofty heroes and heroines out of history or Hollywood. Spouse, in-laws, coworkers, and new friends may be added next, to be replaced later in life by children, children's friends and in-laws, and eventually, grandchildren, each group making its own input to the acculturation process* (1974: 93).[6]

Family photograph collections provide another modern source of influence, another agent of socialization and acculturation. In some instances, parents admittedly recognize the value of having pictorial information about the past available to children. Chiko's daughter, Nancy Herrera Ortiz, said: "I like the memories of . . . where we see each other grow older and then for the kids too—I mean, there's lots of times just like the pictures of my grandfather [Yaichi]—they'll never know my grandfather, not unless you keep pictures and let them know. Same way with my dad's side of the family, they would never have known them so we have pictures of them."[7] As such, important types of information and messages are being transmitted from generation to generation in ways that are taken for granted, that operate alongside the conscious awareness of family members. We are finding that statements of identity and belonging are embedded in these messages.

Other studies have indicated that a child's intense curiosity for his or her parents' past emerges when looking at the family photograph collection (Chalfen 1987). Children seem to be actively searching for answers to questions they have about who their parents and grandparents were in "the old days," what things looked like before they were born, and related matters of personal interest. This may be all the more valid for children of immigrant families. An example comes from Daniel Okimoto's *American in Disguise* when he describes learning about his parents as they were in Japan—of the details of their early years, expulsion from home, and immigration abroad:

> *Pictures looking as if they had been taken in another century were pulled out of dusty albums, including one of my parents' wedding; my young, dark, intense father stood above my mother who, richly clad in a kimono, sat with her hands resting demurely in her lap, looking of all things like a geisha with her enormous black wig, white powdered skin, and tiny cherry plum of a mouth. Never had I seen my God-fearing mother in kimono, let alone thickly powdered or with lipstick! (1971: 186).*

A related example comes from Monica Sone's *Nisei Daughter* when the author is talking about the wedding of her parents:

> *Years later, when Henry and I came upon their wedding picture in our family album, we went into hysterics over Mother's face which had been plastered white and immobile with rice powder, according to Japanese fashion. Only her piercing black eyes looked alive. . . . [Father] stood stiff and agonized in formal white tie and tails (1953: 7).*

It would logically follow that photograph collections take on additional significance to members of immigrant families—families who have participated in such a diversity of past experiences. Family members demonstrate a need to construct an integrated account—one that maintains a sense of continuity by retaining pieces of the past and simultaneously illustrates a process of on-going personal, social, and cultural change.

The Japanese American Family Album Project generated new forms of attention to this integration of continuity, change, and transformation, specifically to cross-generational processes of pictorial communication. When Paul Nagano was talking about how he would like to use his father's photograph collection, he said:

The one thing I'd like to pass on is that they [our children, the next few generations of Japanese Americans] feel really good about who they are in terms of their ethnicity—that they would never feel it's too bad that they're not something else. Don't you think so? You almost do that through osmosis in a way, but that's one thing I'd sure like to pass on, to feel good at who you are, all of your background. Your history there. . . . This idea of preserving is something that has been a little bit more developed after getting involved in this [family album] project. I didn't think of it [at first] in terms of preserving through the photos and journals. I just thought in terms of the the whole identity quest. But I can see that [all] these [photographs and questions] have a bearing on that identity.

We reported earlier, Steve Nagano valued his grandfather's collection as a "cord"[8] that ties families together, and as a way "to remember, record, and share the frozen moments in the past, giving continuity and understanding to future generations."

Continuing Diaristic Habits in Photographic Forms

It is dangerous to make too many generalizations from just the Nagano and the Uyeda/Miyamura photograph collections. Both are rich in imagery, and one is exceptional in its captioning. However it is indeed tempting to speculate on the relationship of album-making to diary-writing, and the possibility that members of some cultures may be more inclined than others to "keep track of themselves" in this manner.

Here we find another example of what people can bring to photography—in this case, knowledge of their ancestors' record-keeping habits. The Japanese government required all families to keep personal histories as a means of political control. During the Tokugawa period (1603–1868), as a means of curtailing conversion to Christianity, the government developed a family registration policy. Every household in Japan was required to register their names with a Buddhist temple. Official notice of affiliation was renewed annually: "The Buddhist temple was chosen partly because it provided an administrative structure capable of handling the registration and supervision of the population" (Smith 1974: 21). In this way, the government coerced the writing of official records of household structure and kinship ties. The point is that detailed record-keeping became a habit, dictated by the state; families had to write down the basic outline of their family history. Personal diary-writing done on a voluntary basis seemed to fill in the blanks between the annual renewal of registration. My speculation is that if cameras had been available in 1640, pictures would have become part of these registration procedures.

In Japan, the diary has become a major literary form since the Heian period (794–1185), and its most noted practitioners have been women (Smith and Smith 1984: 9). We found that the frequency of diary-writing and diaristic documentation are frequently cited themes in the literature on Japanese culture. Robert Smith also noted that diary keeping continues to be quite common in Japan, and "the *nikki* of the famous and infamous alike occasionally are edited for publication. . . . Sometimes a diary kept by a person of less consequence will appear in serial form in a newsletter or magazine, often to be issued later as a book" (Smith and Smith 1984: 8).[9] Smith has also mentioned that Japanese teachers give young students diary-writing assignments as part of their schoolwork. With specific reference to the adoption of photography, Smith added:

> *I do know that the Japanese took to photography very early, as the number of old pictures in various archives shows. What makes this especially interesting, I think, is that there is no Pre-Meiji precedent. . . . [T]he Japanese never took over the "ancestor portrait" in pre-modern times, so the photograph is not a substitute for anything.*

It seems logical to claim that photographic record-keeping is a "natural" extension of this cultural trait, one that might either supplement diary writing or perhaps replace it.

Beyond statements that amateur interest in photography "flourished" in the late 1850s, I have not been able to find documentation of when nonprofessionals began making their own photographs for personal and family use, or when amateur home-mode forms of photography attracted any significant amount of popular attention. However, in one account, we read: "Albums in the possession of Tokugawa Yoshinobu (a lineal descendant of the last shogun) contain hundreds of photographs of this period taken by the brother of Keiki (the last shogun)" (Worswick 1979: 138).

Reverend Paul Nagano contributed the following to our discussion of diary and journal-writing:

> *I was just talking to a [Japanese American] man this morning, and he said, as people retire, there are five things they should do. One is, preserve a journal for the next generation. Isn't that good? And then, the second, maintain a clear mind—like study, you should read a lot, get involved in discussions, it keeps your memory going. And third, identify with movements or organizations of service, where you can be involved in a service type organization. And then, keep in touch with people. The worst thing that can happen is isolation, or just living with your spouse or someone significant. Just living with one person is dull. You gotta get involved with your community some way. . . . And, then, of course, physical exercise. . . . Fine prescription for those who are retired. And I just take the notes down as I talk to him. I thought, "Hey, that's really great."*

This statement describes a lot of what has emerged from our project, and, in part, it explains why Paul has been so supportive throughout our work. We get a better understanding for why Paul confesses a pride in how his son Steve wants to learn so much about the family's past.

The Value of Insiders' Views

Throughout our discussions, we have tried to emphasize that we were breaking new ground by examining family album photography as personal statements—pictorial statements generated by ordinary people as they used "ordinary" cameras, as part of everyday life. We can be certain that these photographers and album-makers did not realize their pictures would be looked at in these ways—either in this theoretical perspective or by strangers. They certainly did not anticipate their photograph collections would become part of "research" for an exhibition sponsored by the National Endowment for the Humanities or for a full-length discussion in book form. Their photographic habits were not coerced by outsiders (with the exception of camera confiscation, as noted); they just went ahead and did what they did. Our task has been one of interpreting what was done, in some senses, trying to explain what we found, and how most of it makes sense. In an attempt to remain consistent, we asked several members of families in the project to say in their own words how they understood what we were doing.

The significance of listening to the many and diverse ways that people have of speaking about themselves continues to attract scholarly attention. Interestingly, anthropologists have always been sensitive to this approach. However, to date, many forms of indigenous expression as parts of social and cultural history remain obscured and virtually unknown. But other problems have been caused by the selective eye and tastes of both academic scholarship and agents of various wings of the publication industry. Certain groups of people and certain expressive forms seem to have counted more than others; minority group expression has often been passed over in favor of attention to representatives of the dominant culture—as in forms of vernacular expression. This has led to an underrepresented account of diversity and sometimes to an unfortunate misrepresentation of cultural behaviors, habits, customs, and so on. To claim that some minority groups have remained "quiet," or "mute" or generally unimpressive begs several important questions—questions that focus on communication. More to the point, it becomes increasingly important to recognize the existence of alternative voices and discourses, sometimes in nonverbal, pictorial forms. Throughout, our claim has been that pictorial representation, even in what some might call "vernacular" forms, should be acknowledged as a legitimate and significant addition to the human repertoire of expressive means—as a way the ordinary people "write" both history and culture (Clifford and Marcus 1986). The Naganos and the Uyeda/Miyamuras clearly demonstrate that ordinary people also "picture" culture. The lesson is that room must be made for "multiple voices" and for alternative interpretations from both the inside and the outside.

Another form of insider's view is produced when an insider is asked to review the research project and results. One family member, Reverend Paul Nagano, was very articulate when he was asked to comment on our study. With specific reference to making identifications of people, places, and activities seen in the Nagano photographs, Paul said:

> *This idea of preserving is something that has been a little bit more developed after [we] got involved in this project. I didn't think of it in terms of preserving through the photos and journals. I just thought in terms of the whole identity quest. But I can see that these all have a bearing on that identity. . . . I think you folks are going to find out a lot of things that will be very informative to us.*

Paul offered us many valuable insider views on Japanese American identity. He took a much broader perspective when we had the following discussion toward the end of our project:

> *RC: I just want to ask you one general question. As you know of our project, how do you see it as a significant project? Either with regard to yourself or to other peoples, or even the general idea of why the project might be important.*
>
> *Paul Nagano: My immediate response is that by the year 2000, the central focus will be in the Pacific Rim, whether it be in terms of economics, politics, and from where I am, it's the ideological or theological perspective, and we don't get enough exposure as Asian people in the United States., whether its our textbooks, or whether it be in terms of any photo exhibit, or journalism books, or whatever. We don't get enough exposure. Everything is Euro-Western. And I think we need to flood the images and minds of the people, particularly on the West Coast with the Asian [populations], and those things are taking place in the Pacific Rim. And the history of the Japanese Americans as a bicultural people. And the other words which I often use is, we have what you might call the "amphibious skills." And by amphibious I mean [the] way we can penetrate the Western dominant group, and communicate—whereas not many people can do that. And at the same time we do have enough of our understanding of what's happening in Asia,*

to be able to be a bridge in terms of communication. So that, an exhibit like this, and anything having to do with Asian-Americans is very important at this juncture in history. And this project will be one of the feeding contributions along that line . . . we need to make as great an impact as possible. . . . Every opening we have, any exposure . . . that's what I want, to catch the vision, that we have a vital, responsible, strategic offering to make, at this juncture.

We have proposed that personal photography encourages us to establish identities in terms of our relationships to social groupings, personal affiliations, and cultural memberships. I am reminded of Adair's comment, cited earlier, that projects like this can give "the individual, family, and community a sense of self-respect—of perpetuating family and community tradition through the use of visual means."

Herein lies the central cue as to why people feel their personal photographs are so important. Photograph collections and family albums produce reassuring looks at life—they reaffirm the sense of belonging to various groups. It is a reintegration and reinterpretation of identity—who, what, and where you've been in light of the present. For purposes of our project, this spells out the process of ethnicity—not a static but a dynamic process of maintaining selective features and characteristics of the past and present with an eye toward the future. This perspective is echoed by anthropologist Michael M. J. Fischer when he states that recent study, thinking, and writing on ethnicity emphasize:

first, *the paradoxical sense that ethnicity is something reinvented and reinterpreted in each generation by each individual and that it is often something quite puzzling to the individual, something over which he or she lacks control. Ethnicity is not something that is simply passed on from generation to generation, taught and learned; it is something dynamic, often unsuccessfully repressed or avoided. . . . Insofar as ethnicity is a deeply rooted emotional component of identity, it is often transmitted less through cognitive language or learning (to which sociology has almost entirely restricted itself) than through processes analogous to the dreaming and transference of psychoanalytic encounters* (1986: 196).[10]

The process of ethnicity involves an "assessment" of traditions (which ones to highlight, include, and exclude)—a form of reinterpretation and, indeed, creation, of traditions.

Illustrated Lives and Pictorial Traditions

New developments in camera technology are promoting the emergence of instant pictorial traditions for peoples all over the world. Memory is being aided and probably reorganized in new ways. I would not claim that family contexts of oral and written traditions are disappearing in all cultures. But it is clear that such forms as diary-writing and story-telling are now accompanied by the production and accumulation of boxes and volumes of personal pictures made by ordinary people. Verbal renditions of life are being supplemented by visual and pictorial means of recording and holding onto the past. Autobiography and biography may be guided more by the pictures that are available than by written or spoken words that used to tell the story. In short, we now live with many possible versions of our own lives—many voices and means of articulation are available.[11] But, it appears that versions of human existence increasingly appear as pictorial lives. The advent of home video-making technology will undoubtably accelerate this process.

Throughout these chapters we have suggested that the family albums in our study may be treated as "immigrants' accounts," as reports, as unconsciously structured interpretations of life, as personal biographies and autobiographies. These versions of life have resulted from an interaction of the Japanese past and the American present—at times of both picture-taking and album organization. We see these behaviors as an active model of participation rather than a passive one. In these ways, a people's home-mode photography can be understood as a construction of "tradition" by "reconceptualizing the past in relation to the meaning of their actions in the present, thereby transforming past and present in a dialectic of interpretation" (Yanagisako 1985: 2). In short, we have looked for photographic evidence that illustrates this active construction of tradition. We have just begun to discover how cameras, used by ordinary people, and personal photographs can contribute to the ways that people fashion traditions as a creative amalgam of continuity and change. We have seen how people are the active agents in the construction of tradition, creating interpretations of the past which incorporate, adapt, or change the models which are familiar to them and provide an acceptable version of life for contemporary times.

Through studies like these we are gaining a better understanding of what the Family Album represents as a medium of intrapersonal, interpersonal, small group communication as well as a cultural document serving the needs of social continuity and integration. We are arriving at a clearer understanding of similarities and differences across different social groups and cultures. As anthropologist John Adair stated, "We don't need a MGM $1 million budget to produce *Roots*. This stuff is found in family albums."

The family album presents a positive view of life and family, generally with an upbeat, progressive tone. The details and specific examples people use to communicate this positive view may differ according to sociocultural circumstances. In order to understand the meaning of dissimilar examples, it is necessary to understand how cultural views differ. It is also important to understand what pictorial possibilities and conventions influence the choices that structure the family album as a message form.

We have seen how a collection of Japanese American albums offers us a wealth of information about individual, social, and cultural contexts of human existence. These pictorial renditions of life are remarkable in detail and perspective. For example, George's use of detailed captions helps teach us where to begin to make meaningful interpretations of what we see. Although such extensive notes and captions are not usually found in family albums, they serve as useful instructions for decoding and analyzing the significance of noncaptioned examples. The Nagano materials have assisted us in interpreting a personal code of communication.

In a broader context, the making of a family album conforms to a habit characteristic of the human condition. Somehow, we persist in finding ways of purposefully depositing evidence of our human existence. From the painting of hand prints in the caves of Lascaux, to the crude tourist expression "Kilroy was here," to planting a flag on the moon, we seem to have an affinity for leaving evidence of ourselves. Historically, this has been the province of the political, aristocratic, or otherwise influential elite. However, the making of snapshots, family albums, and now home videotapes allows ordinary people to do the same. We have seen how carefully and thoughtfully the Nagano and Miyamura/Uyeda families have communicated this evidence of life to present and future generations of their families. We have attempted to celebrate the significance of their family albums and their photographic communication in the writing of this book.

Appendix A

Methods for Studying
Family Photograph Collections

Several types of personal and group interviews were done to gather as many different types of information as possible. Some interviews were done by an oral historian, a visual anthropologist, the project director and assistant director, and even by a member of one Japanese American generation with members of another generation. For instance, we conducted a series of oral history interviews with principal members of the Los Angeles and Gallup families. In other cases we interviewed family members as they reviewed specific pictures in their family albums. These "photo-interviews" served several useful functions. For instance, we elicited information on content—pieces of information that would only be known and remembered by family members, perhaps by the original photographers or current picture custodians. We also noticed that answers to interview questions about photographic content led to a variety of topics, some of which had nothing to do with a specific image but nonetheless were relevant to more general concerns of the research. For instance, an individual photograph might stimulate the telling of family stories, or, in some cases, provoke viewers into a variety of emotional responses and reactions to the photographs. In these ways, we were using photographs as an elicitation device, as part of field methods described best by Collier and Collier (1986). These interviews were very important because we constantly sought to uncover "what they saw"—to enter and understand the personal meanings people attached to their photographs, what they interpreted as significant in their own photographs. In some cases these interviews served as a cross-check on the information developed from oral histories, interviews, and informal discussions with individuals and their families.

The original tape recordings were preserved as archival materials for possible use in additional research or as sound accompaniments to other exhibition forms. Duplicate tapes were made for family members and for study by project staff. Although we obtained complete release statements for all taped and pictorial materials, project policy has restricted release of any of this personal material without explicit permission of family members.

After initially inspecting each photograph collection, family members were asked for permission to borrow and photocopy selective parts of the collection. In some cases this included several albums or individual "bundles" of photographs. The objective was to minimize the loan time as much as possible. Family members may worry about potential loss or damage to their materials during this period, and all precautions were taken to alleviate these concerns, to help build and reinforce a sense of trust.

Whenever possible, family members were asked to sign a release form, giving the project director permission to use their photographs for specific purposes outlined in the project. The family was reassured that they would be consulted throughout the project and asked to approve the use of their materials before exhibition or publication.

In the course of our research we developed methods of copying, inventorying, retrieving, and studying family photographs. As quickly as possible we made facsimile copies of each album with high-quality photocopying technology. The original material was then returned to the homes and care of their custodians. After the first facsimile copies were made, each photograph or item in an album was given a catalog number. This numbering system was organized to differentiate each family, each album, and each kind of collection (shoebox, drawer, wall display), and each photograph. Attention to this kind of catalog system is extremely important when trying to retrieve specific images from a total collection of several thousand pictures.

In some cases it was necessary to produce a translated transcript of captions, notes, and other types of annotations written on album pages or individual photographs. Sometimes the language required the help of a translator; in other cases a member of the family was consulted to read a particularly difficult passage of handwriting.

We then proceeded to make a second generation of facsimile albums. All these copies included the catalog numbers, and, as such, they formed the core of our data base and working documents. While we noticed that image quality deteriorated with each successive copy, first- and second-generation duplicates held sufficient detail and clarity for certain kinds of descriptive and analytical tasks. This method facilitated immediate identification and recognition of materials by different members of the staff, and enhanced the development of description, comparison, and analysis. For instance, these copies were used for detailed notations as new information emerged from either interview materials and/or from other photographic materials supplied by the family. These copies allowed different members of the project, living in different parts of the country, to work on the same materials when they could not meet in person. Other uses of duplicated albums included preparations for exhibition design, pictorial annotation of oral histories, and types of content analysis that required frequency counts of image types and image content.

The next step was to make high-quality photographic copies of each album page and each item (including nonphotographic materials) that appeared on each page. Both color slides and black-and-white negatives were shot at this time. Again, these copy shots, their negatives, and proof sheets were all labeled with the same numbering system used for the facsimile album copies. Each kind of copy proved very useful for different tasks. For instance, the facsimile album pages were studied for research findings and exhibition planning; the slides were used to illustrate lectures about the project and in the production of a videotape that accompanies the traveling exhibition; the prints were included in the exhibition, public relations materials, brochures, newspaper articles, and other professional publications, including, of course, this book. In addition, prints were given as valuable and important presents to family members.

The next stages of work included the identification of image content

—people, places, events, activities, and, in general, a reconstruction of the personal and social circumstances surrounding the production of pictures in the study. Circumstances included identifying who took the photographs, who made the choices of what to shoot and what to keep, who organized the album, and what happened to pictures after they were taken. Of course the interpretation of these findings with reference to cultural context remains as the main challenge. The results of this approach appear in Chapters Three, Four, and Five.

Kinship Charts for Two Families

The Nagano Family

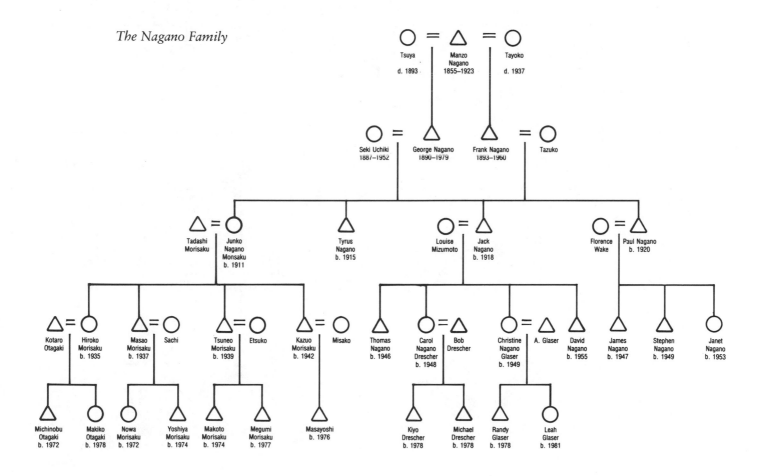

*Reflects research up to 1989

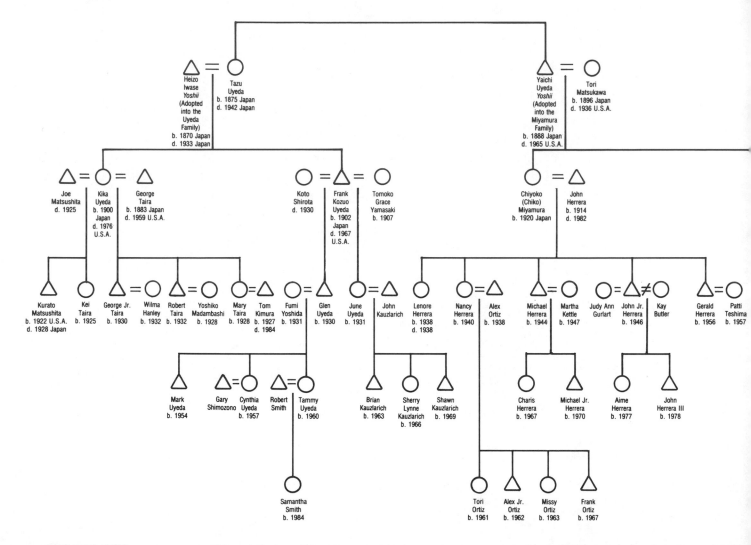

*Reflects research up to 1986

The Uyeda/Miyamura Family

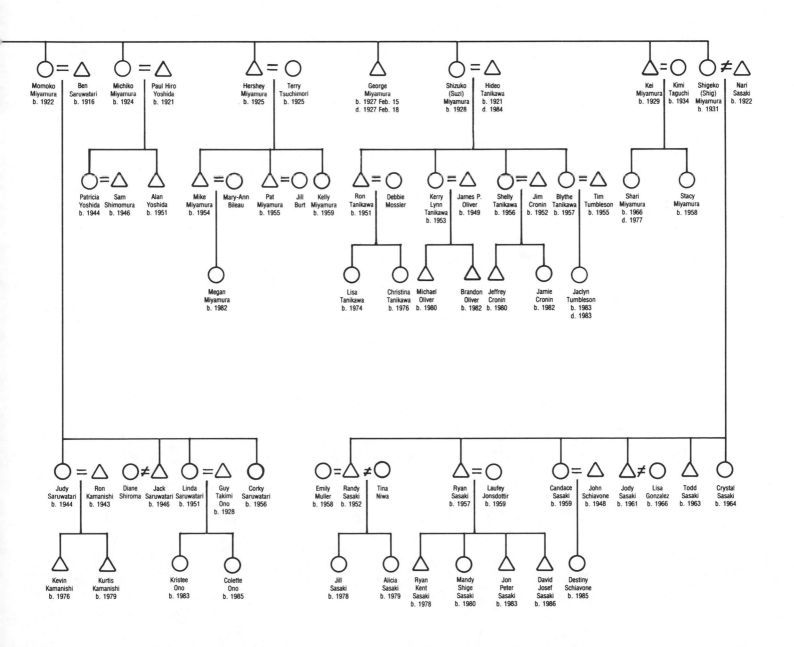

Notes

Preface

1. Akemi Kikumura mentions that picture bride marriages were extensions of legal and social customs established in Japan: "Since the time when photography was introduced in Japan, the exchange of photographs of prospective spouses was a customary first step in the process of arranged marriages that were aided by go-betweens. The actual physical presence of either spouse was not a necessary legal procedure in marriage. Legal status was acquired after the bride's name was placed in the family registry. However, in response to the exclusionists in America, who condemned picture-bride marriages as an immoral practice, the Japanese government stopped issuing passports to picture brides on February 29, 1921" (1981: 113).

2. In one very unusual example, Toyo Miyatake smuggled a lens and film holder into the Manzanar camp, located in Owens Valley, California. He proceeded to construct a crude wooden box camera to fit this lens. Being discovered after nine months, Miyatake convinced authorities of the historical significance of the pictures he made with his camera. He was then allowed to send to Los Angeles for his studio apparatus and darkroom equipment, and, in 1943, he was officially appointed camp photographer for Manzanar (Howe, Nagatani, and Rankin 1978: 9–10).

Chapter One

1. Uchida, Yoshiko *Desert Exile: The Uprooting of a Japanese American Family* (1982: 19).

2. The exploration of photography took place coincidentally with Emperor Meiji's (1867–1912) effort to modernize Japan: "The government needed a great deal of Western technical knowledge. It dispatched students abroad to acquire new skills and hired Western experts at great expense to come to Japan. In these efforts, the Japanese were carefully selective, utilizing the specific national model they felt was best in each field" (Reischauer 1977: 83). It may also be that some of the interest in photography was spurred in Japanese American communities by a lively and internationally known group of photographers. For instance, the Japanese Seattle Camera Club included some of the foremost creative photographers of the Pictorial Movement, and Toyo Miyatake was a famous international photographer before he settled in Los Angeles in the 1920s (Lynne Horiuchi, personal communication, 1989).

3. *The Wolfman Report*. Latest estimates also indicate that approximately 94 percent of these photographs were prints, and that 98 percent were in color (Lydia Wolfman, personal communication, 1988). For a discussion of these figures, see Chapter Two of *Snapshot Versions of Life* by Richard Chalfen (1987).

4. The term *amateur photographer* has come to have several meanings, including early, and often independently wealthy, travel photographers or contemporary camera club photographers, among others.

5. Byers (1966) asks us to attend to how photographers, their subjects, and viewers are related to one another and also to the photographic products per se. Berger and Mohr elaborate upon this triangle of relationships by suggesting that "a photograph is a meeting place where the interests of the photographer, the photographed, the viewer, and those who are using the photograph are often contradictory. These contradictions both hide and increase the natural ambiguity of the photographic image" (1982: 7)

6. For a discussion of how these specific moments add up to "the decisive half minute" in family photography, see Chapter Four of Chalfen's *Snapshot Versions of Life* (1987).

7. It is possible, however, to cite a few international studies, e.g., Erno Kunt's work with Hungarian peasants (1983, 1984), Mihaly Hoppal's study of Hungarian Americans (personal communication), Pierre Bourdieu's classic work in rural France (1965), Yannick Geffroy's recent

study in France (personal communication), Ricabeth Steiger's project with her own family in Switzerland (personal communication), Boerdam and Martinus's research in Holland (1980), and Lynn Blinn's study of Japanese families living in Texas (1986).

8. This concept of ordering a photograph collection may be more complicated than initially expected. For instance, "organized" according to whom? And, to what degree? Again, informal manners and methods of ordering may be important in some contexts and inconsequential in others. Collections might be ordered chronologically by event (e.g., all birthdays of the same person, all Christmas photographs, all vacations, etc.), or just gathered in boxes labeled "Bill's pictures," "Old Country," etc. In still other cases, the photographs might be shuffled like a deck of cards before a new game. Furthermore, people's standards for "organized" may differ with regard to individual personalities, as in the compulsive perfectionist, or other factors such as age or personal life events (e.g., death in the family, a remarriage, the birth of grandchildren, and the like). I hasten to mention also the potential of conflicts in what an outsider-observer may discern as order in comparison to what an insider-participant may claim as order.

9. Several additional points deserve brief mention in conjunction with using "family album" as a central unit of observation and study. First, while family albums are generally composed of photographs, they may also take on features of a scrapbook. Albums frequently contain a variety of other personally valued items, usually referred to as souvenirs or mementoes. These items symbolically represent important times, places, and people that have been experienced in pleasurable ways in past times. Examples may include ticket stubs, printed invitations, newspaper clippings, matchbook covers, postcards, certificates, ribbons, and even locks of hair. George Nagano's album demonstrated how a collection of such materials can be creatively organized into a detailed narrative.

10. While a family album may comprise primarily photographic images, we must also acknowledge that both nonprofessional and professional photographs may be included in the same album. For instance, studio examples may include individual or family portraits, shot from Bachrach Studios to Penney's or Sears Roebuck department stores; we may find wedding portraits, athletic team photographs, portraits

of children with Santa Claus, machine-made or photo-booth pictures, passport photographs, as well as pictures made by street photographers working at popular tourist locations, on-board cruise ships, and elsewhere. In addition, album-makers may include photographic materials clipped from newspapers, magazines, or brochures. This variety of pictorial forms can be quite impressive once we start making an inventory of possibilities.

11. This remark comes from a 1984 study conducted by sociologist Lynn Blinn in which she examined the photograph albums belonging to fifteen upper-middle-class Japanese families living in Houston, Texas. The husbands were doing business for Japanese trading companies. All families had been in the United States for four years and planned to stay no longer than five years. The Japanese term for company people who come to the U.S. for three to five years is *Kaisha*.

12. For an attempt to discover an etiquette of Anglo American photographic habits, see "The Sociovidistic Wisdom of Abby and Ann: Toward an Etiquette of Home-mode Photography" (1984) by Richard Chalfen.

13. In her 1984 study of Japanese family photographs, Blinn stated that "the greater commitment to an identity, the more pictures there will be that represent and reinforce that image. Or the higher the placement of an identity on the hierarchy [of personal or family identities], the more evident it will be in family pictures" (1986: 21).

14. This line of speculation is not unlike expectations suggested by John W. Connor in his book *Tradition and Change in Three Generations of Japanese Americans:*

> *The problem of this investigation as originally stated, was to investigate certain psychological and behavioral characteristics in three generations of Japanese Americans in the Sacramento area in order to determine the degree to which the various generations have retained certain characteristics which are distinctively Japanese or have replaced them with those which are distinctively American. The distinctively Japanese characteristics were grouped under the major headings of hierarchy, collectivity, duty and obligation, deference, and dependence, The distinctively American characteristics were grouped under the major headings of equality, individualism, rights and privileges, self-assertion, and self-reliance (1977: 295).*

I am not presenting these findings as right or wrong; these value group-ings remain problematic for many social scientists and for the people to whom they refer. It is indeed tempting to paraphrase Conner's comment for direct application to our family album project and the Japanese American materials. However, considerable caution is required. This proposal is almost too neat a program or statement of expected re-sults, one which might originally have been a model for the research. Much more time and fieldwork, and much more of an empirical ori-entation would have been needed. Our case study methods were more appropriate given the meagre amount of previous research available for comparison.

15. Another study, done by John Connor on Japanese Americans living in Sacramento, California, also examined the significance of gen eration in relation to ethnic identity:

> *The Ethnic Identity Questionnaire, then, reveals both a considerable attitudinal acculturation in the Issei [first] generation and a consider-able attitudinal ethnicity in the Sansei [third] generation. The term "attitudinal" is deliberate in that . . . the Issei remain psychologically and behaviorally Japanese. Conversely, while the Sansei are psycho-logically and behaviorally closer to the Caucasians than are the Issei or Nisei [second generation], their attitude is also one of seeing a need for the preservation of a Japanese ethnic identity. However . . . those aspects of a Japanese identity that the Sansei wish to preserve are more the artistic and aesthetic rather than the psychological and behavioral . . . (1977: 221–22).*

In another reference, Kiefer offers an additional definition of "genera-tional personality" as follows:

> *We have seen how culture and history interact with the peculiar de-velopmental problems of each generation to produce unique genera-tional personalities. For the issei, the problem is largely a matter of maintaining a sense of connectedness and wholeness in their ebbing lives, and they turn to their traditional culture, for the most part, where they find many solutions. Their developmental success depends to a large extent on having around a social network that considers such solutions sound. The main problem of the nisei is that they have based*

their adjustment to a bicultural environment on the achievement of in-strumental goals with the result of great self-suppression. They are now moving into a stage of life where self-awareness and expressive values will become much more important, and they may have to change their style. The sansei appreciate the difficulties surrounding the nisei style of adjustment and are looking for something better. But in an environ-ment of such abundance, the searchers can easily get lost. The sansei are culturally susceptible to indecision and self-doubt (1974: 228–29).

16. However, more scholars seem to be less and less comfortable with a strict adherence to this generational distinctiveness, associated details, and generalizations. Ethnocentric stereotypes have developed from the delineation of these separate generations. These distinctions are less clear and useful today, in recent examples of immigration, than they were originally when Japanese Americans applied these terms to themselves. Changes in historical context must be kept in mind—in part because U.S. immigration laws changed after 1924. In recent ex-amples, only rarely does a family fit neatly into this model—children may be born to parents that come from different generations; increas-ing instances of ethnic intermarriage, and the like. Current attention seems to be focused more on intragenerational variation.

17. This selection of variables should not overlook questions asso-ciated with reference to the history of photography. We soon realized that some questions cannot be answered without information on his-torical, social, and cultural context of camera use in contexts of every-day life. For instance, what are some of the technological constraints on photography by Japanese Americans during different generational time periods? What new opportunities were made available to amateur photographers as technology and photographic supplies improved? Did it make any difference? How important was advanced technology to nonprofessional photographers taking pictures of family and friends as part of home life?

Chapter Two

1. Case study methods are also preferred when there is more interest in stimulating new insights and speculations than in formally testing

hypotheses and axioms generated from previous work. Clearly, we were not attempting any kind of comprehensive survey based on either selective or random sampling. Nor were we constructing arguments based on quantitative methods supported by statistical measures and data. In contrast, we have carefully stated exactly who we were working with, how we went about our work, and how we reached our conclusions. Our qualitative orientation provided opportunity for discussions of alternative explanations for what we found, a chance to reveal a spectrum of hidden cultural assumptions and more general speculations on relationships among society, culture, and technology.

Case study methods usually produce a rich variety of data. In addition to all the photographs, we collected a rich array of spoken material, including direct verbatim commentary from personal interviews, comments from life histories, group interviews, and casual conversations. Only a small portion of this information was organized for use in the traveling exhibition. This book is taking advantage of the quantity and quality of findings that resulted from the case studies done in Los Angeles and Gallup.

2. Organizing the study in this way promoted a comparison of photographic materials based on an implied significance of interethnic diversity. Models of ethnic and generational identity of Japanese Americans have been developed from studies that concentrated on people living in large urban West Coast centers such as Los Angeles (Kitano 1976), the San Francisco area (Kiefer 1974), Seattle (Yanagisako 1985), and Sacramento (Conner 1977). However it is clear that the Japanese American experience extends beyond the confines of the urban setting, and that the heterogeneity of the Japanese American experience deserves equal time and attention.

In our choice of families, and in our statement of findings, we tried to be careful about making facile and simplistic generalizations. This is particularly inappropriate from case study materials. For instance, we make no claims for what *all* Japanese Americans do with their photographs or what they think about photographic representation. We have tried *not* to imply that there is *one and only one* model of what it means to be Japanese American. We have sought a better understanding of what "Japanese American" means. Our case study design has probed particular features and characteristics of different Japanese American experiences. Here I call attention to such variables as: (1) interaction with other ethnic groups, minority groups; (2) employment in non-Japanese businesses; (3) intermarriage with other ethnicities; (4) membership in non-Japanese organizations; (5) amount of staying in touch with or seeing parents; (6) number of return trips to Japan; (7) practice of Japanese customs associated with Japanese holidays; (8) respect for the deceased or special birthdays, among others. Examples of this diversity appear when Conner notes differences between Japanese Americans living in Seattle vs. Sacramento; when Kiefer sees differences between San Francisco's Tokyo Town and elsewhere; and when several authors caution the clumping of Hawaiian and mainland groups of Japanese Americans. (For a relevant discussion, see Conner 1977: 104.)

3. Information on this accounting has been collected from several sources. We had personal interviews with three of George's four children and one of his grandsons, Steve Nagano. We were also fortunate to have several tape-recorded interviews with George. In addition we have spent many hours examining this rich collection of images, their captions, and other contents of George's album.

4. This statement appeared as part of the exhibition text for *Japanese American Family Albums: A Los Angeles Family* which opened at the Japanese American Culture and Community Center in Los Angeles on February 20, 1983.

5. For a discussion of immigration and mining in Wyoming, Colorado, and Utah, see Wilson and Hosokawa 1989: 93–95.

6. For a discussion of the ecomomic relationships among boarding-houses and railroad recruitment, contractors, agents, and their fees, see Wilson and Hosokawa 1989: 73–74.

7. However, after World War II, there was considerable geographical dispersement of Miyamura family members, sometimes for reasons of schooling, military service, or marriage. Four of the Miyamura Nisei settled in the Los Angeles area.

8. But interethnic variability may even be greater than major differences in geographic region might suggest. For instance, Chiko discussed some variation even within Japanese American communities in the Southwest. She brought up differences between Gallup and Winslow, where she felt Japanese Americans stayed much more to themselves, and even stayed in closer touch with West Coast peoples, especially in

matters of banking and purchases of goods, etc.

9. Malcolm Collier has suggested as a correlated project the need to see if photographs were also saved or put into albums by their Anglo, Mexican, Italian, Hispanic, and Native American friends in Gallup. This approach might further clarify certain cultural preferences for saving pictorial information and further develop patterns of pictorial communication (personal communication 1988).

Chapter Three

1. Malcolm Collier notes that while he hears of this practice in personal interviews with Japanese Americans, he has not seen captions used this way in a sample of their more recently made family photograph albums. Collier has been able to review many photograph albums made by Asian American families as part of a college course he offers at the San Francisco State University entitled "Photo Exploration of Asian America." He felt that George Nagano's album has an extraordinary amount of personally written text (captioning), detail, and organization on an explicit level. Collier added that (1) "virtually the only albums with text that have come through my class have been Japanese American"; and (2) the Japanese American albums seem to be more elaborately and deliberately constructed than albums made by other Asian American groups, including attention given to dating photographs, precise positioning and page layout, and strict chronological order (personal communication, 1988).

2. The Mayfair Hotel was located close to other Japanese boardinghouses adjacent to Little Tokyo, Los Angeles. Manzo was one of the first Issei to establish a boardinghouse for Japanese workers in North America. In this way, George was practicing a trade he may have known through his father's experience.

3. One additional example comes from Monica Sone's *Nisei Daughter* when she was describing an incident in 1941:

> *FBI agents come to the Matsui house looking for Mr. Matsui:*
>   *"Why you mix 'em all up? He not home, not home." . . . One man brought his face down close to hers, shouting slowly and clearly,*
>   *"WHERE IS YOUR HUSBAND? YOU SAID HE WAS IN HERE A MINUTE AGO!"*
>   *"Yes, yes, not here. . . . Such stupid men."*

> *Mrs. Matsui dove under a table, dragged out a huge album and pointed at a large photograph. She jabbed her gnarled finger up toward the ceiling, saying, "Heben! Heben!"*
>
> *The men gathered around and looked at a picture of Mr. Matsui's funeral. Mrs. Matsui and her two children were standing by a coffin, their eyes cast down, surrounded by all their friends, all of whom were looking down. The three men's lips formed an "Oh." One of them said, "We're sorry to have disturbed you. Thank you, Mrs. Matsui, and good-bye." They departed quickly and quietly (1953: 154).*

4. In a section of *Country Voices: The Oral History of a Japanese American Family Farm Community* entitled "Snapshot, 1944," David Mas Masumoto describes a Japanese American's thoughts while looking at a photograph of a funeral:

> *I stare at the silent and still faces, expressions frozen in a snapshot. My family stands to the right,* Jitchan *holds a flag,* Baachan *lifts a photograph of her dead son. . . . It was my Uncle's funeral in 1944 at someplace called Gila River Relocation Center, Arizona. . . .* Baachan *clutches the photograph of her dead son. . . .* Baachan *lifts the gold framed picture, her dark hands curled around the edges as she elevates it slightly, trying to hold it steady between herself and* Jitchan. *. . . Silent expressions locked in a snapshot.* Jitchan *and* Baachan *clutch the remains of their dead son. Dad stands in the blurred background.*
>
> *I do not and cannot know what they felt. I was born ten years later in a different time and place. But a silence penetrated such gaps, linking me with my past: a silence felt by my family and carried through the years; a silence that teaches yet I do not fully understand; a silence captured for a moment in a snapshot, 1944 (1987: 54, 56, 58).*

5. Malcolm Collier finds that the display of personal photographs of deceased family members in photo albums, on household walls, in shrines, on graves, or as part of funeral processions is not isolated to Japanese American examples—such practices are familiar to other Asian American groups as well. He adds that he does not find funeral snapshots in recently made albums and suggests considerable variation may exist across Asian American groups. For instance, Collier states that while cameras have not been present in the Chinese Ameri-

can memorial services he has attended, his Vietnamese students report people taking photographs at funerals, including shots of the deceased (personal communication, 1988).

6. This album was made by the Nakai family and is currently held in the archival collections of the Balch Institute of Ethnic Studies in Philadelphia.

Chapter Four

1. Hershey Miyamura's accomplishments have become a significant part of Japanese American history. In Bill Hosokawa's book, *Nisei: The Quiet Americans*, we read:

> *One other* Nisei *has won the Medal of Honor. He is Sgt. Hiroshi "Hershey" Miyamura, who served briefly with the 442nd. Recalled into service for the Korean War, he was a member of the 7th Infantry Division when his company was attacked near Taejon-ni the night of April 24, 1951. His citation reads: "Corporal Miyamura, a machine gun squad leader, aware of the imminent danger to his men, unhesitatingly jumped from his shelter wielding his bayonet, hand-to-hand combat, killing approximately 10 of the enemy. Returning to his position, he administered first aid to the wounded and directed their evacuation as another savage assault hit the line. He manned his machine gun and delivered withering fire until his ammunition was expended. He ordered the squad to withdraw, while he remained behind to render the gun inoperative, He then bayoneted his way through infiltrated enemy soldiers to a second gun emplacement and assisted in its operation. When the intensity of the attack necessitated the withdrawal of the company, Corporal Miyamura ordered his men to fall back while he remained to cover their movement. He killed more than 50 of the enemy before his ammunition was depleted and he was severely wounded. He maintained his magnificent stand despite his painful wounds, continuing to repel the attack until his position was overrun. When last seen, he was fighting ferociously against an overwhelming number of enemy soldiers.*
>
> *Miyamura was captured and spent 29 months in a North Korean camp. Only after he was repatriated was it announced he had won the Medal of Honor. President Eisenhower decorated him in ceremonies at the White House in 1954 (1969: 413).*

2. Yanagisako makes a similar finding: "Sisters, moreover, are the kin keepers who facilitate communication, coordinate gift exchanges, and bring kin together. . . . Gift-exchange plans among sisters sometimes approach the elegance of structuralist societies. Nisei sisters and their mothers are also the organizers of what are referred to as 'family gatherings' (1985: 217). More will be said of family gatherings and reunions in Chapter Five.

3. For instance, Yanagisako notes: "The affinal extension, in turn, is an outcome of attempts by Nisei couples . . . to bring together in one gathering both their respective "sides of the family"—that is, each spouse's parents, siblings, and their spouses and children, or what might be called their inclusive natal conjugal family" (1985: 223). Yanagisako gives examples of how kin assemblages from each side of the family fluctuate or alternate from one holiday gathering (e.g., Thanksgiving, Christmas) to the next. This might be expected all the more in communities like Gallup where outmarriage was more common than larger Japanese American communities on the West Coast.

4. This is a *kinen shashin* photograph—a commemorative photograph taken of important events. Here Tori is holding her six-month-old daughter, just before they were to leave Japan for Gallup, New Mexico. This type of photograph conforms to our observations of celebrating last times and farewells found in the Nagano materials. Malcolm Collier has noted that "departure shots" taken at the Hong Kong Airport or at the docks are quite common in Chinese American albums brought into class by his students.

5. In *All Japan: The Catalogue of Everything Japanese,* the authors make references to reunions in a section entitled "Ritual Travel": "[It] is not unusual for men in their eighties to attend reunions of their elementary school classes" (1984: 169). Among Japanese Americans, the Redress movement created the opportunity for the organization of a number of "camp" reunions. Now that the Nisei are in retirement there have been many reunions attended by people that have been in contact or known about each other for more forty years. The "camp" experience has definitely been a factor in creating common friendships and community networks.

6. However, the exchange of personal photographs may not always be accepted. In *Nisei Daughter,* Monica Sone describes an incident

that reminds us of comments Chiko made about her school friends and some of Frank's and Yaichi's pictures:

> *On my last day at Central Grammar School, romance burst into my life. During the hubbub of graduation, Haruo, the handsomest boy in the class and the top athlete, jammed a white envelope into my hands with a hurried farewell.*
>
> *"Here, this is for you Kazuko. Good luck, and I'll write you from Franklin High."*
>
> *The envelope contained a snapshot of himself. Although I was so thrilled I could have floated right off into space, I stood staring helplessly at the picture, not knowing what to do with it. I wanted to put it in a beautiful frame and display it on top of the piano at home, but I knew that would bring an avalanche of disapproval upon my head from my parents. I also knew I could not hide it, for no matter where I put it . . . Sumiko, the family explorer, would find it, and triumphantly show it to Mother and Father, who would deal with me from then on. No, I simply could not risk taking the snapshot home.*
>
> *I took one last adoring look at it. Haruo looked wonderful in his white school sweater. A lock of black hair fell carelessly over his high forehead and he was grinning from ear to ear. Slowly I tore the glossy picture into tiny pieces and let them flutter into the wastebasket (1953: 125).*

Sone does not elaborate on this type of restriction. This example illustrates the power of social context in determining meaning and use of something as "innocent" as the snapshot image. Also, we see that having a photograph of someone (image content and image possession) can have several meanings and consequences; details of social context again play an important role.

7. The status of the eldest male in Japanese household is made clear by Glenn when she states:

> *The ie was hierarchically structured according to three principles of stratification: gender, age, and insider-outsider status. Males took precedence over females, older people over younger, and those born in the household over those born outside it. . . . The head of the household*

was usually the eldest male born in the household, who thereby had the high status on all three grounds and was accorded ultimate authority (1986: 202).

Chapter Five

1. In this regard, several aspects of photographic context become important. Contextual features surrounding personal appearances in photographs are being understood as intentional, as a preferred way of making an appearance in photographic form, and not as purely accidental. Identifications of specific locations, backgrounds, or surroundings, as well as of people and things in the picture, become important to this type of analysis. Thus, close-up pictures of individual people and faces, devoid of background or surroundings, are less useful than medium shots, long shots, or wide-angle views. The importance of context also includes instances when annotations have been added or other pictorial or written materials are found associated with individual photographs. This has been illustrated in our analysis of the Nagano materials. And, finally, this contextual perspective applies to examining how photographs are juxtaposed on individual album pages or are included in the same album. Our comments on the Uyeda/Miyamura collection demonstrate the significance of this idea.

2. There are limitations, however, because photographic conventions must be accounted for as a form of constraint. We cannot expect to find all personal and social relationships represented in these photograph collections. Different groups of people may not share the same habits for appropriate picture-taking—that is, for when and where pictures should or might be taken. For instance, I have seen my own teenage daughters take many snapshots of their girlfriends and occasionally boyfriends. However, their male counterparts do not seem to initiate this activity. Idiosyncratic differences must also be taken into account —to understand examples of extraordinarily unusual behavior, much more so than people like George Nagano, Yaichi Miyamura, or Frank Uyeda who became so enthusiastic about taking pictures.

3. I located this family album in the archives of the Balch Institute for Ethnic Studies in Philadelphia. It was donated to the library by Yone Okamoto in 1976. The Okamoto family lived in the Philadelphia area from the 1910s to 1975; the family had been interned at Heart

Mountain Relocation Center, Wyoming, in 1942–43.

4. This material is also located in the library of the Balch Institute in Philadelphia. The Nakai family immigrated to California and was interned in Poston, Arizona; in 1948 they relocated to Seabrook, New Jersey.

5. Modell also mentions that as "early as 1914 the Southern California (Christian Japanese) Church Federation established a department of social work with a full-time employee. From tasks like teaching English, sewing, and 'Americanization,' and attacking (in 1915) the rise of organized gambling in Little Tokyo, they progressed to serving those members who, without families to support them, were hard hit by the Depression" (1977: 76–77).

6. Modell continues by offering an interesting contrast: "The Buddhist Temple Association, founded only in 1925, was concerned mainly with enforcing a degree of orthodoxy in doctrinal matters, for several unorthodox sects had begun to spring up in the American environment. In contrast, Christian interdenominational cooperation was more concerned with proselytizing and social service" (1977: 77).

7. To further confuse this situation, due "to an 'integration' move in Christian churches, Japanese Christian Churches have removed the 'Japanese' designation, and have adopted names that make it difficult to identify them as ethnic churches. Many Japanese Americans now attend churches with non-Japanese designations" (Waugh, Yamoto, and Okama 1988: 170).

8. Kieffer offers us additional context on team activities: "with the gradual growth of the nisei population, games and sports became an important avenue for status competition not only among the nisei participants but among the spectators—their issei parents. Kitano . . . describes a community picnic: 'During the races and competitive games that take place throughout the afternoon, much store is set on winning. It is important that a man's son be better than other men's sons, and the spirit of the games is more serious than one might find at an Iowa sack race.'

As the nisei grew, organized leagues for team sports became a salient feature of the community and in fact one of the major group activities. Competition between nisei teams—especially basketball teams—became a way of life for many boys" (1974: 18).

9. For a description of a community picnic from the oral history of

a farm community in Del Rey, California, see Masumoto (1987: 99–106). The author comments on tradition and change as seen in lists of contributions and menus for these picnics.

10. Lili Sasaki describes life in camp, first at the Santa Anita Relocation Center, then at Amachem, California:

> *And of course, Japanese love clubs. We were clubbed to death in all the*
> *camps: sewing clubs and poetry clubs and this and that. Right away,*
> *we put together a writers' club, artists' club. Even an exercise club.*
> *I could get up in the morning, and I could hear them exercising. The*
> *Japanese are organizers, right away they are organizing (Gesensway*
> *and Roseman 1987: 104).*

11. It should be remembered that George's album celebrates his marriage to Seki, hence the title "Nagano's Mother 1910–1952." As discussed in Chapter Two, George and Seki's first child and only daughter, Junko Nagano, while born in Canada, lived in Japan between 1911 and 1965; clearly she was not as much a part of the Nagano family as the three boys, Tyrus, Jack, and Paul. George did add pictures of Junko to his album after 1965.

12. Smith notes that in Kurusu, Japan, "The high point of summer is the three-day observance of *o-bon*, the Festival of the Dead. Like the New Year Celebrations, it has for centuries been an occasion when it is hoped that scattered family members can come back to the countryside, visit the graves of the ancestral dead, and share in a joyous reunion" (1978: 158).

13. Just as Bon can be cited as an example of transformation, the same might be said of *Koden* which also focuses on notions of reciprocity and belonging. Yanagisako notes that *Koden* or mortuary offering "is another medium through which sibling sets affirm their continuing presence as a family in the Japanese American community" (1985: 227). The Nisei view *Koden* reciprocity as a Japanese custom governed by Japanese rules (1985: 234). *Koden* in rural Japan consisted of exchanging fixed quantities of rice or other edible goods. Again, change, adaptation, and transformation can be seen. For example, Yanigisako mentions that "in Japanese American communities *Koden* consists of relatively fixed amounts of money that are used to pay the high costs of the funeral" (1985: 227). This version of *Koden* may even involve

exchanges between friends and associates as well as kin.

14. Assistant director of our project, Elizabeth Chestnut, has suggested that these photographs are best understood as a form of "visual or pictorial *ohakamairi*," as personal photographs that enhance the linkage of the living to the recently departed and ancestors.

Chapter Six

1. The statement reads as follows: "*Kodak culture* will refer to whatever it is the one has to learn, know, or *do* in order to participate appropriately in what has been outlined as the home mode of pictorial communication. As in most studies of culture, we are exploring ideas, values, and knowledge that are informally or unconsciously learned, shared, and consensually agreed upon in tacit ways by members of society—in this case, by ordinary people who use their cameras and pictures as part of everyday social life" (1987: 10). In a related version, anthropologist Margaret Blackman refers to the "culture of imaging" as follows: "the patterns of behavior and beliefs brought to the making, viewing and understanding of photographic images, something quite apart from a study of the cultural content of the image itself" (1981: 45).

2. Barbara Rosenblum describes alternative models of work within professional photography in her book *Photographers at Work* (New York: Holmes & Meier, 1978).

3. Film scholar James Potts raises several interesting questions along these lines:

> It seems unlikely that the use of an Arriflex camera automatically imposes a Teutonic film style, that an Eclair gives Gallic flair, or that by toting a Japanese Super 8mm. camera with a power zoom one starts perceiving the world through the eyes of an Oriental (however "Westernized"). But it is becoming generally accepted that technology is not value-free: to some extent different technologies dictate the way in which we see the world, the way we record and interpret "reality," and they influence the types of codes we use to communicate a message (1979: 74).

4. In Robert Smith's book on Japanese culture entitled *Kurusu,* he describes the contemporary situation as follows:

What kind of view do the young have of their past? It is probably no more or less distorted than that of any other group of similar age, and they were fascinated by the photographs I had taken twenty-five years before. Since cameras, now [1978] so common, were rather rare in those days, they had never seen photographs of their parents when they were young. They exhibited what must be universal amazement at being presented with irrefutable evidence that twenty-five years before their mothers had been straight-backed and smooth skinned and their fathers' faces had been less lined and their eyes clearer. They were also struck by the material changes in Kurusu (1978: 197).

5. Most photograph albums still require some form of written or spoken accompaniment to perform these tasks successfully. That is, the pictures need some forms of contextual information. Malcolm Collier has reminded me that "this communication is often hampered by the relatively low context content of much family photography—lacking the necessary memory holders to add the context—the albums can become very enigmatic, even to family members. In this context, George's extensive texts can be seen perhaps as a planned attempt to overcome these limitations!" (personal communication, 1988).

6. In another context but equally as relevant, Yanagisako also leaves room for roles of personal and public media: "people do not simply learn a traditional system of ideals, symbols, metaphors, and norms about the family and kinship from conservative agents of cultural transmission inside the family and a modern system from progressive agents of cultural transmission outside it, but rather that they construct notions of 'traditional' and 'modern' from what they are told by *all agents of cultural transmission* and what they experience both inside and outside families" (1985: 257, emphasis added).

7. News Release, Maxwell Museum, University of New Mexico, February 27, 1984.

8. The cord metaphor is also used by Christie Kiefer in a similar reference to continuity:

These ideas are part of a vast and subtle difference between the Japanese and American cultures—a difference in the whole perception of self and time. The traditional Japanese view sees the individual life as a single segment of a continuous cord. Life and its circumstances are

gifts from countless prior generations, whose repayment flows on to the
generations of the indefinite future (1974: 185).

9. When Robert Smith reviewed our initial speculations on the importance of diary-keeping and album-making, he commented:

> *As for record-keeping in Japan, it is positively a mania and has been*
> *for centuries. I don't know what else to say about it, except that as an*
> *example, I can tell you that from the mid-seventeenth century to 1868,*
> *there were annual censuses of the commoner population, and in the*
> *archives there are innumerable registers of land, domesticated animals,*
> *swords, firearms, etc., etc.* (personal communication, September 1982).

10. Fischer has revealed how expressions of ethnicity can be found in autobiographical fiction—"Autobiography was chosen because, like ethnography, it has a commitment to the actual" (1986: 198). What he says of autobiographical novels might well be applied to the constructions of statements of life found in family albums, here with special attention to the future: "What thus seem initially to be individualistic autobiographical searchings turn out to be revelations of traditions, recollections of disseminated identities and of the divine sparks from the breaking of vessels. These are a modern vision of the Phagorean arts of memory: retrospection to gain a vision for the future" (1986: 198).

11. For a thought-provoking treatment of the interaction of memory and family photographs, home movies and related artifacts made by a Japanese American family, see *Family Gathering*, a half-hour film by Lise Yasui (Chalfen 1989). This film is distributed by New Day Films and was nominated for an Academy Award in 1989.

Bibliography

1. Japanese and Japanese American References

Befu, Harumi
    1965   "Contrastive Acculturation of California Japanese: Comparative Approach to the Study of Immigrants" in *Human Organization* 24: 209–16.

Benedict, Ruth
    1946   *The Chrysanthemum and the Sword*. New York: Meridian Books.

Berrien, F. K., Abe Arkoff, and Shinkuro Iwahara
    1967   "Generation Difference in Values: Americans, Japanese-Americans, and Japanese" in *The Journal of Social Psychology* 71: 169–75.

Caudill, William, and Henry A. Scarr
    1962   "Japanese Value Orientations and Culture Change" in *Ethnology* 1: 53–91.

Chalfen, Richard
    1989   "Review of *Family Gathering*" in *American Anthropologist* 91(2): 525–27.

Condon, John, and Keisuke Kurata
    1974   *What's Japanese About Japan*. Tokyo: Shufunotomo Co., Ltd.

Conner, John W.
    1977   *Tradition and Change in Three Generations of Japanese Americans*. Chicago: Nelson-Hall.

Dalby, Liza, et al.

    1984   *All-Japan: The Catalogue of Everything Japanese*. New York: Quill.

DeFrancis, John

    1973   *Things Japanese in Hawaii*. Honolulu: University Press of Hawaii.

Doi, Takeo

    1971   *The Anatomy of Dependence*. New York: Kodansha International, Ltd.

Fudei, Budd

    1976   "That Feeling of Belonging," in *The Japanese American Story*. Minneapolis, Minn.: Dillon Press, pp. 120–29.

Gesensway, Deborah, and Mindy Roseman

    1987   *Beyond Words: Images from America's Concentration Camps*. Ithaca, N.Y.: Cornell University Press.

Glenn, Evelyn Nakano

    1986   *Issei, Nisei, War Bride: Three Generations of Japanese American Women in Domestic Service*. Philadelphia: Temple University Press.

Hosokawa, Bill

    1969   *Nisei: The Quiet Americans*. New York: William Morrow.

Hsu, Francis L. K.

    1970   *Iemoto: The Heart of Japan*. New York: Schenkman Publishing Co.

Ichihashi, Yamato

    1969 [1932]   *Japanese in the United States*. New York: Arno Press.

Ito, Kazuo

    1973   *Issei: A History of Japanese Immigrants in North America*. Seattle: Japanese Community Service.

Kiefer, Christie W.

    1974   *Changing Cultures, Changing Lives: An Ethnographic Study of Three Generations of Japanese Americans*. San Francisco: Jossey-Bass Publishers.

Kikumura, Akemi

    1981   *Through Harsh Winters: The Life of a Japanese Immigrant*

Woman. Novato, Ca.: Chandler & Sharp Publishing.

Kikumura, Akemi, and Harry H. L. Kitano

1981   "The Japanese American Family," in *Ethnic Families in America—Patterns and Variations* (2nd ed.), Charles H. Mindel and Robert W. Habenstein (eds.). New York: Elsevier, pp. 43–60.

Kim, Elaine H.

1982   "Japanese American Family and Community Portraits," in *Asian American Literature: An Introduction to the Writings and their Social Context*. Philadelphia: Temple University Press, pp. 122–72.

Kitano, Harry H. L.

1976 [1969]   *Japanese Americans: The Evolution of a Subculture* (2nd ed.). Englewood Cliffs, N.J.: Prentice-Hall.

Lebra, Takie Sugiyama

1976   *Japanese Patterns of Behavior*. Honolulu: University Press of Hawaii.

Leighton, Alexander H.

1946   *The Governing of Men*. Princeton, N.J.: Princeton University Press.

Levine, Gene N., and Colbert Rhodes

1981   *The Japanese American Community: A Three-Generation Study*. New York: Praeger.

Lukes, Timothy J., and Gary Y. Okihiro

1985   *Japanese Legacy: Farming and Community Life in California's Santa Clara Valley*. Local History Series Vol. 31. Cupertino, Ca.: California History Center.

Lyman, Stanford

1970   "Generation and Character: The Case of the Japanese Americans," in *The Asian in the West*, S. Lyman (ed.). Reno: University of Nevada Press, pp. 81–97, 161–68.

Masumoto, David Mas

1987   *Country Voices: The Oral History of a Japanese American Family Farm Community*. Del Rey, Ca.: Inaka Countryside Publications.

Modell, John
    1977   *The Economics and Politics of Racial Accommodation: The Japanese of Los Angeles, 1900–1942*. Urbana: University of Illinois Press.

Montero, Darrel
    1980   *Japanese Americans: Changing Patterns of Ethnic Affiliations Over Three Generations*. Boulder, Co.: Westview Press.

Nakane, Chie
    1970   *Japanese Society*. Berkeley: University of California Press.

Okimoto, Daniel I.
    1971   *American in Disguise*. New York: Walker Weatherhill.

Peterson, William
    1971   *Japanese Americans: Oppression and Success*. Washington, D.C.: University Press of America.

Reischauer, Edwin O.
    1977   *The Japanese*. Cambridge, Ma.: Harvard University Press.

Shinazaki, Toson
    1976   *The Family*. Translated and with introduction by Cecelia Segawa Seigle. Tokyo: University of Tokyo Publications.

Sone, Monica
    1953   *Nisei Daughter*. Boston: Little, Brown.

Smith, Robert J.
    1983   *Japanese Society*. New York: Cambridge University Press.
    1978   *Kurusu: The Price of Progress in a Japanese Village, 1951–1975*. Stanford: Stanford University Press.
    1974   *Ancestor Worship in Contemporary Japan*. Stanford: Stanford University Press.

Smith, Robert J., and Kazako Smith (eds.)
    1984   *The Diary of a Japanese Innkeeper's Daughter*. Translated by Miwa Kai. Cornell University East Asia Papers, No. 36.

Uchida, Yoshiko
    1982   *Desert Exile: The Uprooting of a Japanese American Family*. Seattle: University of Washington Press.

Waugh, Isami A., Alex Yamato, and Raymond Y. Okamura
    1988   "Japanese Americans in California," in *Five Views: An Ethnic*

Sites Survey for California. Sacramento, Ca.: Office of Historic Preservation.

Yanagisako, Sylvia Junko

1985 *Transforming the Past: Tradition and Kinship Among Japanese Americans*. Stanford: Stanford University Press.

II: Photography References

Barthes, Roland

1981 *Camera Lucida*. New York: Hill and Wang.

Bellman, Beryl, and Bennetta Jules-Rosette

1977 *A Paradigm for Looking: Cross Cultural Research with Visual Media*. Norwood, N.J.: Ablex.

Beloff, Halla

1985 *Camera Culture*. Oxford: Basil Blackwell Ltd.

Berger, John, and Jean Mohr

1982 *Another Way of Telling*. New York: Pantheon Books.

Blackman, Margaret

1981 *Window on the Past: The Photographic Ethnohistory of the Northern and Kaigani Haida*. Mercury Series, Ethnology Service Papers 74. Ottowa: Canadian National Museum of Man.

Blinn, Lynn

1986 "Japanese Family Photos: Propositions about Family Identity." Paper presented during the Fourth International Conference on Visual Sociology, Bielefeld, West Germany.

Boerdam, Jaap, and Warna Oosterbaan Martinus

1980 "Family Photographs: A Sociological Approach," *The Netherlands Journal of Sociology* 16(2): 95–119.

Bourdieu, Pierre, et al.

1965 *Un Art Moyen—Essais sur les Usages Sociaux de la Photographie* (2nd ed.). Paris: Les Editions de Minuit.

Byers, Paul

1966 "Cameras Don't Take Pictures," *Columbia University Forum* 9: 27–31.

Chalfen, Richard

    1988   "Home Video Versions of Life—Anything New?," *Society for Visual Anthropology Newsletter* 4(1): 1–5.

    1987   *Snapshot Versions of Life: Explorations of Home Mode Photography*. Bowling Green, Oh.: The Popular Press.

    1984   "The Sociovidistic Wisdom of Abby and Ann: Toward an Etiquette of Home Mode Photography," *Journal of American Culture* 71(1–2): 22–31.

    1983   "Exploiting the Vernacular: Studies in Snapshot Photography," *Studies in Visual Communication* 9(3): 70–84.

    1981   "A Sociovidistic Approach to Children's Filmmaking: The Philadelphia Project," *Studies in Visual Communication* 7(1): 2–32.

Coe, Brian, and Paul Gates

    1977   *The Snapshot Photograph: The Rise of Popular Photography, 1888–1939*. London: Asch and Grant, Ltd.

Collier, John, Jr., and Malcolm Collier

    1986   *Visual Anthropology: Photography as a Research Method* (rev. ed.). Albuquerque: University of New Mexico Press.

Geffroy, Yannick

    1987   "Family Photographs: A Visual Patrimony." Unpublished ms., files of the author.

Graves, Ken, and Mitchell Payne (eds.)

    1977   *American Snapshots*. Oakland, Ca.: Scrimshaw Press.

Green, Jonathan (ed.)

    1974   *The Snap-Shot*. Millerton, N.Y.: Aperture.

Hirsch, Julia

    1981   *Family Photographs: Content, Meaning and Effect*. New York: Oxford University Press.

Hoppal, Mihaly

    1986   "Ethnic Symbolism and Images of Identity: Family Photography of the American Hungarian." Paper prepared for the 1987 Conference on Family Photography and Cross Cultural Comparison, Utrecht, Holland.

Howe, Graham, Patrick Nagatani, and Scott Rankin (eds.)

1978 *Two Views of Manzanar: An Exhibition of Photographs by Ansel Adams/Toyo Miyatake*. Los Angeles, Ca.: Frederick S. Wight Art Gallery, University of California, Los Angeles.

Kaufmann, James

1980 "Learning from the Fotomat," *The American Scholar* 49(2): 244–46.

King, Graham

1984 *Say "Cheese"!: Looking at Snapshots in a New Way*. New York: Dodd, Mead and Co.

Kotkin, Amy

1978 "The Family Album as a Form of Folklore," *Exposure* 16(1).

Kunt, Erno

1984 "Lichtbilder und Bauern: Ein Beitrag zu einer Visuellen Anthropologie ("Photographs and Peasants: A Contribution to Visual Anthropology")," *Sonderdruck aus Zeitschrift fur Volkskunde* 11: 216–28.

1983 "Photography and the Peasant," *New Hungarian Quarterly* 24(96): 13–20.

Lesy, Michael

1980 *Time Frames: The Meaning of Family Pictures*. New York: Pantheon.

Musello, Christopher

1980 "Family Photography" in *Images of Information*, Jon Wagner (ed.). Beverly Hills, Ca.: Sage Publications, pp. 101–18.

Newhall, Beaumont

1982 *The History of Photography from 1839 to the Present*. Boston: Little, Brown.

Ohrn, Karin B.

1975 "The Photoflow of Family Life: A Family's Photograph Collection," *Folklore Forum* 13: 27–36.

Oestreicher, Richard

1981 "From Artisan to Consumer: Images of Workers 1840–1920," *Journal of American Culture* 4(1): 47–64.

Perkins, Stephen E.

1982 "Toward an Alternative History of Photography." Master's thesis, San Francisco State University.

Potts, James

1979 "Is There an International Film Language?," *Sight and Sound* 48(2): 74–81.

Schwartz, Dona B., and Michael Griffin

1987 "Amateur Photography: The Organizational Maintenance of an Aesthetic Code" in *Natural Audiences: Qualitative Studies of Media Uses and Effects*, Thomas R. Lindlof (ed.). Norwood, N.J.: Ablex.

Seiberling, Grace, with Carolyn Bloore

1986 *Amateurs, Photography, and the Mid-Victorian Imagination.* Chicago: University of Chicago Press.

Sontag, Susan

1978 *On Photography*. New York: Dell Publishing Co.

Steiger, Ricabeth

1987 "'You Look Just Like Elsa': A Father Photographs His Daughters in the Early Twentieth-Century." Unpublished ms., files of the author.

Taft, Robert

1964 "The Family Album" in *Photography and the American Scene: A Social History, 1839–1889*. New York: Dover.

Thomas, Alan

1977 "The Family Chronicle" in *Time in a Frame: Photography and the Nineteenth-Century Mind*. New York: Schocken Books.

Wolfman, Lydia (ed.)

1984 *The 1983–1984 Wolfman Report on the Photographic Industry in the United States*. New York: ABC Leisure Magazines, Inc.

Worswick, Clark

1979 "Photography in Nineteenth-Century Japan" in *Japan: Photographs 1854–1905*, Clark Worswick (ed.). New York: Pennwick, pp. 129–41.

Worth, Sol, and John Adair

1972 *Through Navajo Eyes: An Exploration in Film Communi-*

cation and Anthropology. Bloomington: Indiana University Press.

III: Other References

Carpenter, Edmund
   1975   "The Tribal Terror of Self-Awareness" in *Principles of Visual Anthropology*, Paul Hockings (ed.). Paris: Mouton Publishers, pp. 451–62.
Clifford, James, and George Marcus (eds.)
   1986   *Writing Culture: The Poetics and Politics of Ethnography*. Berkeley: University of California Press.
Csikszentmihalyi, Mihaly, and Eugene Rochberg-Halton
   1981   *The Meaning of Things: Domestic Symbols and the Self*. New York: Cambridge University Press.
De Vos, George, and Lola Romamucem-Ross (eds.)
   1975   *Cultural Continuities and Change*. Palo Alto: Mayfield Publishing Co.
Fischer, Michael M. J.
   1986   "Ethnicity and the Post-Modern Arts of Memory" in *Writing Culture—The Poetics and Politics of Ethnography*, James Clifford and George E. Marcus (eds.). Berkeley: University of California Press, pp. 194–233.
Goffman, Erving
   1974   *Frame Analysis: An Essay on the Organization of Experience*. New York: Harper Colophon Books.
Gleason, Philip
   1983   "Identifying Identity: A Semantic History," *The Journal of American History* 69(4): 910–31.
Langness, L. L., and Gelya Frank
   1981   *Lives: An Anthropological Approach to Biography*. Navato, Ca.: Chandler & Sharp Publishing.
Reminick, Ronald A.
   1983   *Theory of Ethnicity: An Anthropologist's Perspective*. New York: University Press of America.

Index

Note: page numbers in **bold face** indicate that the reference is in a caption.

Turning Leaves
The Photograph Collections of Two Japanese American Families

Edited by Dana Asbury
Designed by Milenda Nan Ok Lee
Typography in Sabon
by Tseng Information Systems, Inc.
Printed by Thomson-Shore, Inc.
Printed in the U.S.A.